All·You·Need

KOREAN

for Absolute Beginners

**from alphabet,
numbers
to key expressions**

All-You-Need Korean for Absolute Beginners

Written by   Miss Vicky (Hyojeong Shim)
Publisher   Kyudo Chung
Published by   Darakwon

First Published   2024. 6. 25

Editorial Planner   Hyukju Kwon, Taekwang Kim
Editor   Huchun Lee, Chaeyoon Han, Hyoeun Kim

Designed by   SINGTA Design
Illustrated by   Gentle mellow
Video filmed and edited by   Miss Vicky

DARAKWON

Darakwon Bldg., 211 Munbal-ro, Paju-si, Gyeonggi-do, Republic of Korea 10881
Tel : 02-736-2031
Fax : 02-732-2037
(Marketing Dept. ext.:250~252, Editorial Dept. ext.: 291~296)

ISBN   978-89-277-7434-1   13710

http://www.darakwon.co.kr
http://www.darakwonusa.com

Visit the Darakwon homepage to learn about our other publications and promotions
and to download the contents in MP3 format.

All·You·Need

KOREAN

for Absolute Beginners

from alphabet,
numbers
to key expressions

Written by **Miss Vicky**

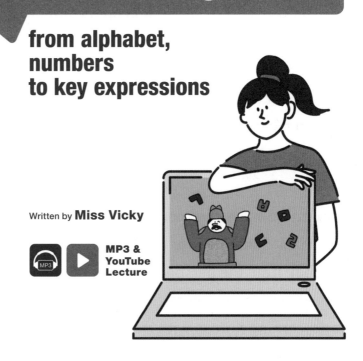

MP3 &
YouTube
Lecture

DARAKWON

Preface

Hello, everyone! My name is Hyojeong Shim, and I'm a native Korean speaker. I teach Korean to non-native learners through videos, website, tutoring and group classes, and I'm most known as Miss Vicky from my YouTube channel, Korean with Miss Vicky.

It's been more than five years since I started teaching Korean, as of the publication of this book. I've always loved English from a young age, and I initially dreamed of becoming a successful English teacher in Korea. However, various turns of events led me to commit to the field of Korean education instead, and I'm grateful for how it turned out. Now I'm dedicated to teaching Korean and plan to continue on this path.

Drawing from the common questions I've received from many students over the years, I've aimed to write this book from the perspective of someone who is just beginning to learn Korean. I believe that anyone who starts learning Korean with this book will gain a better understanding of the Korean language and build a strong foundation, which will undoubtedly remain a valuable asset throughout their learning journey.

This book has three chapters. The first chapter covers Korean alphabets, as mastering the alphabets is the most important first step in learning a language. The subsequent chapters cover simple yet essential topics like basic expressions and numbers.

In every chapter, you'll find useful information that broadens your understanding of the Korean language and answers the questions that may naturally arise as you study. You can approach this book from the perspective of studying, but it will also be helpful to approach it as reading an informative and engaging book about Korean.

I look forward to this book being a special part of your journey, and I wish you an enjoyable and rewarding path toward your goal.

— *Miss Vicky*

How to use this book

기역, 니은,
디귿, 리을,
미음, 비읍…

Video Lessons - QR code

Introduction to Hangeul

LECTURE

Before you start learning Hangeul, there are some basic concepts you should know.

Hangeul is made up of **consonants**(자음) and **vowels**(모음). There are 19 consonants and 21 vowels in total. Korean characters are formed by combining these consonants and vowels.

Hangeul's consonants are categorized into two types: the initial consonants, which are usually referred to as "consonants," and the **final consonants**, which are specifically called 받침. Initial consonants and final consonants can include almost the same consonants, but there's more variety in what can be used for final consonants. You'll explore this in more detail in the chapter on final consonants.

In Korean, consonants always appear first, followed by vowels. Final consonants are placed below the combination of the initial consonant and vowel.

Korean Syllable Blocks

C : Consonant
V : Vowel
F.C : Final Consonant

Each character represents one syllable, and it's required to have both a consonant and a vowel in a syllable. However, a character cannot contain multiple initial consonants or vowels; it can only have one of each.

Some vowels appear next to the consonant, while others go below it. This unique arrangement allows for a wide range of sounds in the Korean language.

Let's take a brief look at all the consonants, vowels, and final consonants on the next page.

Scan the QR code to access the video lessons for Chapters 1 and 3. Using this book alongside the videos will help consolidate your learning.

LECTURE

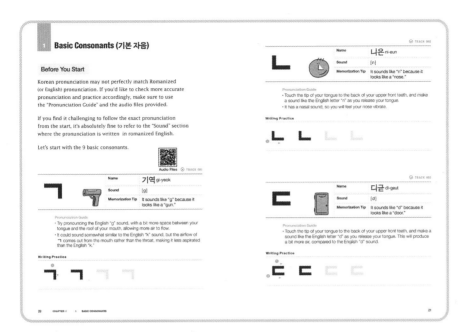

CHAPTER 1

In CHAPTER 1,
you'll learn all the details
about Hangeul, from
consonants, vowels,
final consonants to
consonant assimilation rules,
accompanied by
a thorough explanation
to help you master it.
You can use the
book's writing section to
practice writing each letter,
and also use the provided
audio files to practice
pronouncing them.

Audio Files

Download the audio files
by scanning
the QR code or visiting
the Darakwon USA website
(www.darakwonusa.com).

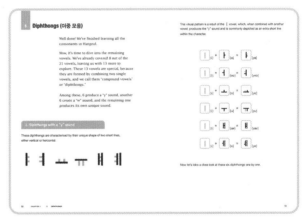

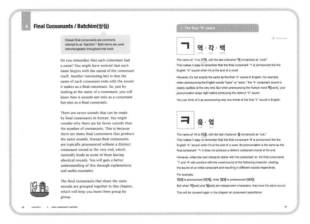

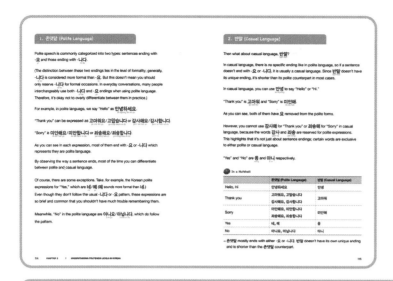

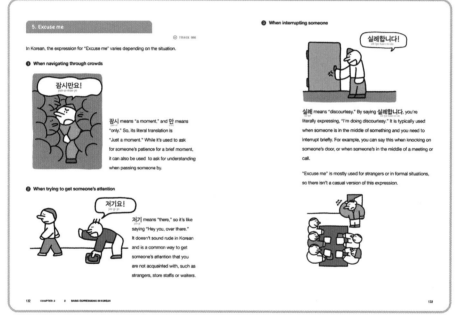

CHAPTER 2

In CHAPTER 2, you'll learn about two different language styles in Korean, polite and casual, along with various basic expressions.
You'll gain an understanding of the appropriate contexts for using each expression in different situations.

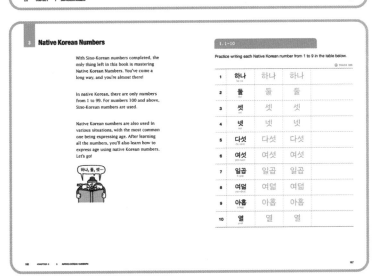

CHAPTER 3

In CHAPTER 3, you'll explore Korean numbers, which come in two types: Sino-Korean and Native Korean.

EXERCISES

Each chapter includes various exercises so you can immediately review the material you've learned. It's highly encouraged to finish all the exercises and mark any incorrect answers for further review during your study sessions.

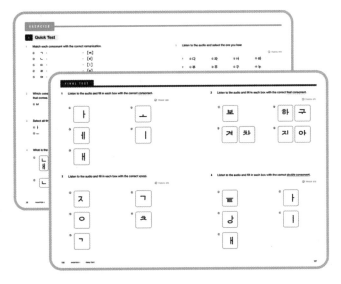

Table of Contents

CHAPTER 1 한글 **(Hangeul, Korean Alphabet)**

CHAPTER 2 존댓말 **vs** 반말
(Polite vs. Casual Language)

CHAPTER 3 숫자 **(Numbers)**

CHAPTER 1

한글
Hangeul, Korean Alphabet

Let's start with Hangeul,
the Korean alphabet.
It's an essential first step in
your Korean journey,
as it lays the foundation for understanding
pronunciation and characters.

Hello, everyone!

Welcome to Chapter 1, and congratulations on embarking on this new journey of learning Korean. I hope you enjoy every step of the way, and that you'll go all the way without giving up.

First and foremost, we'll learn how to read and write "Hangeul," the script used in the Korean language.

Hangeul was invented by King Sejong in the 15th century. At that time, there was no writing system that matched the Korean language, so Koreans had long been using Chinese characters for writing. However, they were mainly used by the ruling class because they were too difficult for the common people to learn. This led to high illiteracy rates, and King Sejong felt compassion for his people.

Over many years, he worked tirelessly to create a writing system that even common people could learn easily. As a result, King Sejong successfully invented what is now known as Hangeul(한글), the Korean alphabet.

Hangeul is known as one of the easiest and most scientific writing systems in the world. Its creator, King Sejong, is famously quoted to have said, "A bright man can acquaint himself with them before the morning is over, and even a dull man can learn them in the space of ten days."

But of course, for non-native Korean speakers, getting familiar with Hangeul will take a bit more time. Also, Korean pronunciation differs from English in many ways, so even after becoming familiar with the characters, adapting to the pronunciation will be another aspect that requires time. This is a common challenge among learners, and you're not alone.

With this chapter, you can learn Hangeul not only with engaging visuals but also through detailed explanations, audio files and numerous exercises. Together, they will help strengthen your memory and make the learning process more effective and enjoyable.

So, shall we start together?

Introduction to Hangeul

LECTURE

Before you start learning Hangeul, there are some basic concepts you should know.

Hangeul is made up of **consonants**(자음) and **vowels**(모음). There are 19 consonants and 21 vowels in total. Korean characters are formed by combining these consonants and vowels.

ja-eum

mo-eum

Hangeul's consonants are categorized into two types: the initial consonants, which are usually referred to as "consonants," and the **final consonants**, which are specifically called 받침. Initial consonants and final consonants can include almost the same consonants, but there's more variety in what can be used for final consonants. You'll explore this in more detail in the chapter on final consonants.

batchim

In Korean, consonants always appear first, followed by vowels. Final consonants are placed below the combination of the initial consonant and vowel.

Korean Syllable Blocks

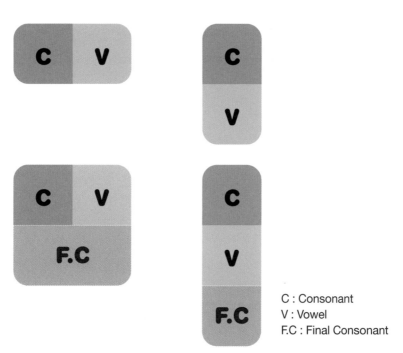

C : Consonant
V : Vowel
F.C : Final Consonant

Each character represents one syllable, and it's required to have both a consonant and a vowel in a syllable. However, a character cannot contain multiple initial consonants or vowels; it can only have one of each.

Some vowels appear next to the consonant, while others go below it. This unique arrangement allows for a wide range of sounds in the Korean language.

Let's take a brief look at all the consonants, vowels, and final consonants on the next page.

Overview of Hangeul

Consonants 자음

Basic Consonants

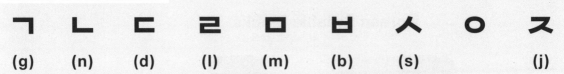

ㄱ (g) ㄴ (n) ㄷ (d) ㄹ (l) ㅁ (m) ㅂ (b) ㅅ (s) ㅇ ㅈ (j)

Aspirated Consonants

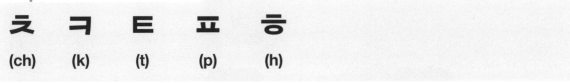

ㅊ (ch) ㅋ (k) ㅌ (t) ㅍ (p) ㅎ (h)

Double Consonants

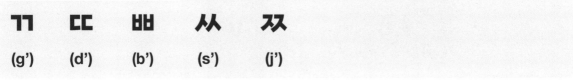

ㄲ (g') ㄸ (d') ㅃ (b') ㅆ (s') ㅉ (j')

Vowels 모음

Single Vowels

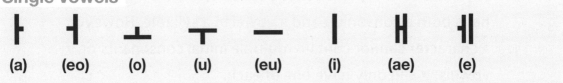

ㅏ (a) ㅓ (eo) ㅗ (o) ㅜ (u) ㅡ (eu) ㅣ (i) ㅐ (ae) ㅔ (e)

Dipthongs (Compound Vowels)

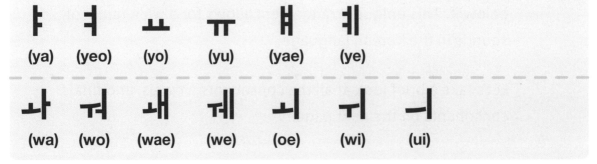

ㅑ (ya) ㅕ (yeo) ㅛ (yo) ㅠ (yu) ㅒ (yae) ㅖ (ye)

ㅘ (wa) ㅝ (wo) ㅙ (wae) ㅞ (we) ㅚ (oe) ㅟ (wi) ㅢ (ui)

Final Consonants/Batchim 받침

Single Batchim

1 **The Final "k" sound**

ㄱ ㅋ

2 **The Final "n" sound**

ㄴ

3 **The Final "t" sound**

ㄷ ㅅ ㅈ ㅊ ㅌ ㅎ

4 **The Final "l" sound**

ㄹ

5 **The Final "m" sound**

ㅁ

6 **The Final "p" sound**

ㅂ ㅍ

7 **The Final "ng" sound**

ㅇ

Compound Batchim

ㄲ	ㅆ	ㄳ	ㄵ	ㄶ	ㄺ	ㄻ
(k)	(t)	(k)	(n)	(n)	(k)	(m)

ㄼ	ㄽ	ㄾ	ㄿ	ㅀ	ㅄ
(l)	(l)	(l)	(p)	(l)	(p)

1 Basic Consonants (기본 자음)

Before You Start

Korean pronunciation may not perfectly match Romanized (or English) pronunciation. If you'd like to check more accurate pronunciation and practice accordingly, make sure to use the "Pronunciation Guide" and the audio files provided.

If you find it challenging to follow the exact pronunciation from the start, it's absolutely fine to refer to the "Sound" section where the pronunciation is written in romanized English.

Let's start with the 9 basic consonants.

Audio Files ⊙ **TRACK 001**

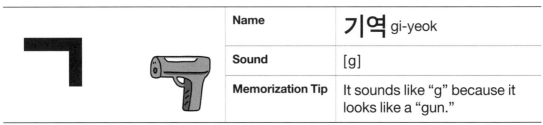

	Name	기역 gi-yeok
	Sound	[g]
	Memorization Tip	It sounds like "g" because it looks like a "gun."

Pronunciation Guide
- Try pronouncing the English "g" sound, with a bit more space between your tongue and the roof of your mouth, allowing more air to flow.
- It could sound somewhat similar to the English "k" sound, but the airflow of ㄱ comes out from the mouth rather than the throat, making it less aspirated than the English "k."

Writing Practice

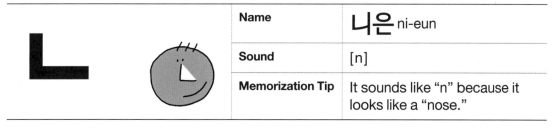

Name	ㄴ은 ni-eun
Sound	[n]
Memorization Tip	It sounds like "n" because it looks like a "nose."

Pronunciation Guide

- Touch the tip of your tongue to the back of your upper front teeth, and make a sound like the English letter "n" as you release your tongue.
- It has a nasal sound, so you will feel your nose vibrate.

Writing Practice

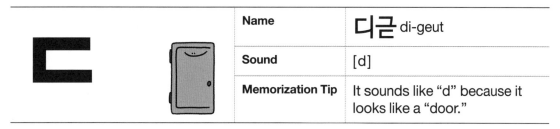

Name	ㄷ귿 di-geut
Sound	[d]
Memorization Tip	It sounds like "d" because it looks like a "door."

Pronunciation Guide

- Touch the tip of your tongue to the back of your upper front teeth, and make a sound like the English letter "d" as you release your tongue. This will produce a bit more air, compared to the English "d" sound.

Writing Practice

Name	리을 li-eul
Sound	[l]
Memorization Tip	It sounds like "l" because it has a "long line."

Pronunciation Guide

- Put the tip of your tongue on the roof of your mouth, behind your upper front teeth. Make a sound like the English letter "l" as you release your tongue.

Writing Practice

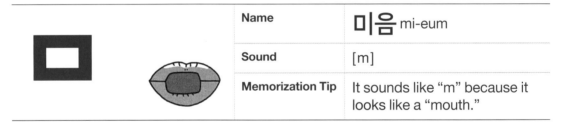

Name	미음 mi-eum
Sound	[m]
Memorization Tip	It sounds like "m" because it looks like a "mouth."

Pronunciation Guide

- Start with your lips closed and lightly touching each other, and then make a sound like the English letter "m" by releasing your lips.
- The lips touch with less pressure compared to when pronouncing the English "m," and they don't fully cover each other.
- It has a nasal sound, so you will feel your nose vibrate.

Writing Practice

Name	비읍 bi-eup
Sound	[b]
Memorization Tip	It sounds like "b" because it looks like a "bucket."

Pronunciation Guide

- Start with your lips closed and lightly touching each other, and then make a sound like the English letter "b" by releasing your lips.
- The lips touch with less pressure compared to when pronouncing the English "b," and they don't fully cover each other. This will produce a bit more air, compared to the English "b" sound.

Writing Practice

Name	시옷 si-ot
Sound	[s]
Memorization Tip	It sounds like "s" because it looks someone is "standing."

Pronunciation Guide

- It is similar to the letter "s" in English, but its pronunciation is more relaxed and weaker. Try making the "s" sound as in the word "stand," but like a hissing sound.

Writing Practice

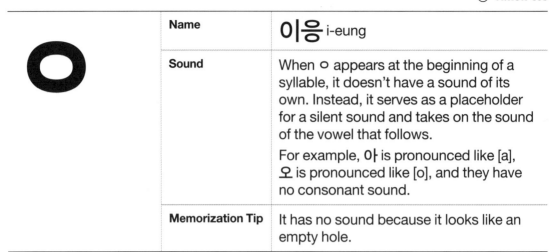

Name	이응 i-eung
Sound	When ㅇ appears at the beginning of a syllable, it doesn't have a sound of its own. Instead, it serves as a placeholder for a silent sound and takes on the sound of the vowel that follows. For example, 아 is pronounced like [a], 오 is pronounced like [o], and they have no consonant sound.
Memorization Tip	It has no sound because it looks like an empty hole.

Writing Practice

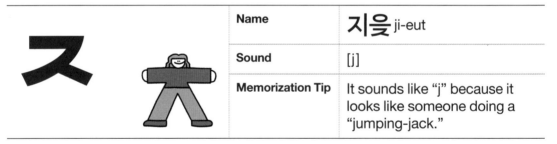

Name	지읒 ji-eut
Sound	[j]
Memorization Tip	It sounds like "j" because it looks like someone doing a "jumping-jack."

Pronunciation Guide

• Touch the tip of your tongue to the back of your upper front teeth, and make a sound like the English letter "j" as you release your tongue. This will produce a bit more air, compared to the English "j" sound.

• You don't need to round your lips. Just pronounce them with your lips apart.

Writing Practice

2 Single Vowels (단모음)

Do you remember when we learned about the consonant ㅇ, how it doesn't make its own sound but follows the sound of the vowel that comes after it? Well, now you might be curious about what vowels there are. Let's learn some of the vowels first before we dive into the rest of the consonants. We will start with the 8 simplest vowels called the "single vowels."

In Korean, the vowels' sounds are typically shorter and more concise compared to English vowels, unless you are speaking slowly for clarity or tone. For instance, in English, vowels can be drawn out in words like "bee" or "say," where the vowel sound is held for a longer duration, but in Korean, they're pronounced more quickly and crisply.

(In the audio, the vowel sound is slowed down and elongated to help learners clearly hear and distinguish each sound.)

As we learned in the introduction, each vowel can be positioned in two different ways: either next to or below a consonant. Vowels with a longer vertical line are placed next to a consonant, while those with a longer horizontal line are positioned below a consonant.

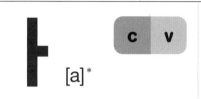 It is placed next to a consonant.

⊙ **TRACK 010**

[a]*

Pronunciation Guide

It sounds similar to the English "ah" sound, as in the word "father," but with less elongation.

Writing Practice

⊙ **TRACK 011**

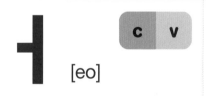
[eo]

Pronunciation Guide

It sounds similar to the English "uh" sound, as in the word "up," but with less elongation.

Writing Practice

* Notations in the brackets are the standardized romanization of each vowel.

It is placed **below** a consonant.

[o]

Pronunciation Guide

- It sounds similar to the English "o" sound, as in the word "go."
- Your lips come closer together and stick out slightly more, and your tongue is positioned in the middle of your mouth. This will naturally create a shorter "o" sound.

Writing Practice

[u]

Pronunciation Guide

It sounds similar to the English "oo" sound, as in the word "food," but with less elongation.

Writing Practice

━━━ [eu]

Pronunciation Guide

Thinly stretch your lips out to the sides, open your lips a bit, and then make a sound. Do not let your teeth touch each other, and make sure that your front teeth are not completely covered by your lips. This will create a sound close to — sound.

Writing Practice

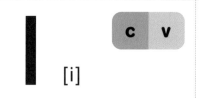

| [i]

c v

Pronunciation Guide

It sounds similar to the English "ee," as in the word "see," but with less elongation.

Writing Practice

Pronunciation Guide

It sounds similar to the English "a" sound, as in the words "cat" or "may," but with less elongation.

Writing Practice

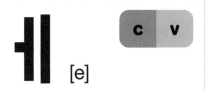

Pronunciation Guide

It sounds similar to the English "e," as in the words "egg" or "edit," but with less elongation.

▶ The difference between ㅐ and ㅔ is that your mouth is slightly more open when pronouncing ㅐ compared to ㅔ, and ㅔ is pronounced with slightly less effort. These are very subtle differences that are hard to distinguish, especially at first. It is generally acceptable to pronounce them the same way.

Writing Practice

EXERCISE

A Quick Test

1 Match each consonant with the correct romanization.

① ㄱ •   • [m]

② ㄴ •   • [d]

③ ㄷ •   • [ㅣ]

④ ㄹ •   • [g]

⑤ ㅁ •   • [n]

2 Which consonant has no sound of its own and follows the vowel sound that comes after?

① ㅂ   ② ㅅ   ③ ㅇ   ④ ㅈ

3 Select all the vowels that are placed <u>below</u> a consonant.

① ㅏ   ② ㅓ   ③ ㅗ   ④ ㅜ

⑤ ㅡ   ⑥ ㅣ

4 What is the correct way to write ㄴ and ㅐ ?

①

②

③

④

5 Listen to the audio and select the one you hear.

⊙ TRACK 018

1   ① 다   ② 라   ③ 사   ④ 바

2   ① 부   ② 무   ③ 구   ④ 누

3   ① 에   ② 네   ③ 메   ④ 제

4   ① 우이   ② 오이   ③ 어이   ④ 아이

ANSWER

1   ① [g]   ② [n]   ③ [d]   ④ [l]   ⑤ [m]

2   ③

3   ③, ④, ⑤

4   ③

5   1. ③   2. ①   3. ④   4. ②

B Writing Practice

1 Combine each consonant and vowel to create a character.

	ㅏ (a)	ㅓ (eo)	ㅗ (o)	ㅜ (u)	ㅡ (eu)	ㅣ (i)	ㅐ (ae)	ㅔ (e)
ㄱ (g)	가	거						
ㄴ (n)	나							
ㄷ (d)								
ㄹ (l)								
ㅁ (m)								
ㅂ (b)								
ㅅ (s)								
ㅇ								
ㅈ (j)								

Practice reading and writing the words in Korean. ⊙ TRACK 019

	거미	거미		그네	그네
spider			swing		
	나무	나무		나비	나비
tree			butterfly		
	다리	다리		도시	도시
leg bridge			city		

	모자	모자		바지	바지
hat, cap			pants		
	버스	버스		새	새
bus			bird		
	아기	아기		오이	오이
baby			cucumber		

Aspirated Consonants (치음 자음)

This time, we're going to learn five more consonants. What distinguishes these five consonants from the others is that they are pronounced with stronger airflow, known as "치음(aspirated sound)."

▶ TRACK 020

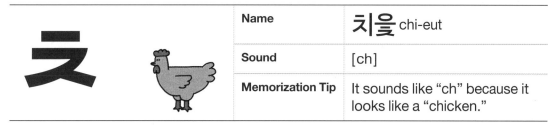

Name	치읓 chi-eut
Sound	[ch]
Memorization Tip	It sounds like "ch" because it looks like a "chicken."

Pronunciation Guide

- ㅊ is pronounced with the same tongue position and mouth shape as ㅈ. The top horizontal line represents a stronger burst of air.
- Touch the tip of your tongue to the back of your upper front teeth, and make a sound like the English letter "ch" as you release your tongue.
- You don't need to round your lips. Just pronounce them with your lips apart.

Writing Practice

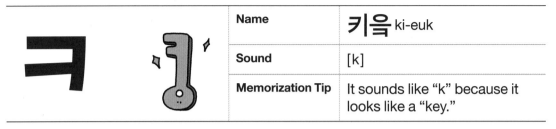

Name	키읔 ki-euk
Sound	[k]
Memorization Tip	It sounds like "k" because it looks like a "key."

Pronunciation Guide

- ㅋ is pronounced with the same tongue position and mouth shape as ㄱ. The extra horizontal line represents a stronger burst of air.
- Try to release more air from the throat as you pronounce ㄱ(g). This will produce a sound similar to the English "k".

Writing Practice

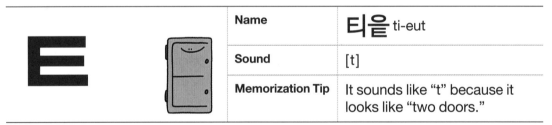

Name	티읕 ti-eut
Sound	[t]
Memorization Tip	It sounds like "t" because it looks like "two doors."

Pronunciation Guide

- ㅌ is pronounced with the same tongue position as ㄷ. The extra horizontal line represents a stronger burst of air.
- Touch the tip of your tongue to the back of your upper front teeth, and make a sound like the English letter "t" as you release your tongue.

Writing Practice

Name	피읖 pi-eup
Sound	[p]
Memorization Tip	It sounds like "p" because it looks like a "pile" of books.

Pronunciation Guide

- ㅍ is pronounced with the same mouth shape as ㅁ and ㅂ. The additional lines represent a stronger burst of air.
- Start with your lips closed and lightly touching each other, and make a sound like the English letter "p."

Writing Practice

Name	히읗 hi-eut
Sound	[h]
Memorization Tip	It sounds like "h" because it looks like a man wearing a "hat."

Pronunciation Guide

- Exhale gently while making a sound similar to "h" in English, as in "hat."

Writing Practice

Consonant Sounds Comparisons

⊙ **TRACK 025**

Sometimes, ㄱ[g] can sound similar to ㅋ[k]. Additionally, ㄴ[n] can sound similar to ㄷ[d], ㄷ[d] to ㅌ[t], ㅁ[m] to ㅂ[b], ㅂ[b] to ㅍ[p], and ㅈ[j] to ㅊ[ch]. These 6 pairs of consonants are the most common source of confusion among learners, and it's a question that learners frequently ask. Here is some guidance on why this happens and how to differentiate each consonant from one another.

① ㄱ vs ㅋ

When ㄱ is at the beginning of a word, there's more puff of air during its pronunciation compared to when it's within a word, sounding somewhat similar to ㅋ.

고구마 **sweet potato**

→ Compare how 고 and 구 sound in this word.

On the other hand, ㅋ releases a stronger burst of air than ㄱ.

가지 **eggplant** 카드 **card**

→ Compare how 가 and 카 sound.

② ㄴ vs ㄷ

When ㄴ appears at the beginning of a word, it is pronounced with more puff of air compared to when it's within a word, sounding somewhat similar to ㄷ.

나비**butterfly** 하나**one**

→ Compare how 나 sounds in each word.

On the other hand, the ㄷ sound is produced with a stronger release of the tongue from your upper teeth and even more puff of air, compared to when pronouncing ㄴ. Additionally, there is no vibration in your nose, unlike ㄴ. (ㄴ is nasal, ㄷ is not).

나비**butterfly** 다리**leg, bridge**

→ Compare how 나 and 다 sound.

③ ㄷ vs ㅌ

When ㄷ appears at the beginning of a word, it is pronounced with more puff of air compared to when it's within a word, sounding somewhat similar to ㅌ.

다시**again** 수다**chatting**

→ Compare how 다 sounds in each word.

On the other hand, ㅌ releases a stronger burst of air than ㄷ.

다시**again** 타조**ostrich**

→ Compare how 다 and 타 sound.

④   ㅁ vs ㅂ

When ㅁ appears at the beginning of a word, it is pronounced with more puff of air compared to when it's within a word, sounding somewhat similar to ㅂ.

모자**hat** 이모**aunt**

→ Compare how 모 sounds in each word.

On the other hand, ㅂ releases much more air than ㅁ. Additionally, there is no vibration in your nose, unlike ㅁ. (ㅁ is nasal, ㅂ is not).

모자**hat** 초보**beginner**

→ Compare how 모 and 보 sound.

⑤   ㅂ vs ㅍ

When ㅂ appears at the beginning of a word, it is pronounced with more puff of air compared to when it's within a word, sounding somewhat similar to ㅍ.

버스**bus** 아버지**father**

→ Compare how 버 sounds in each word.

On the other hand, ㅍ releases a stronger burst of air than ㅂ.

바지**pants** 파리**a fly**

→ Compare how 바 and 파 sound.

⑥ ㅈ vs ㅊ

When ㅈ appears at the beginning of a word, it is pronounced with more puff of air compared to when it's within a word, sounding somewhat similar to ㅊ.

자리**seat** 피자**pizza**

→ Compare how 자 sounds in each word.

On the other hand, ㅊ releases a stronger burst of air than ㅈ.

자리**seat** 차**a car, tea**

→ Compare how 자 and 차 sound.

A Quick Test

1 Match each consonant with the correct romanization.

① ㅊ •   • [k]

② ㅋ •   • [p]

③ ㅌ •   • [h]

④ ㅍ •   • [ch]

⑤ ㅎ •   • [t]

2 What is the correct way to write ㅌ and —?

①
```
ㅌ
—
```

②
```
ㅌ —
```

③
```
—
ㅌ
```

④
```
— ㅌ
```

3 Listen to the audio and select the one you hear.

▶ TRACK 026

1 ① 처   ② 커   ③ 터   ④ 퍼

2 ① 키   ② 티   ③ 피   ④ 히

4 Listen to the audio and fill in the blank with the character you hear.

▶ TRACK 027

1

 조

2

후

ANSWER

1 ① [ch] ② [k] ③ [t] ④ [p] ⑤ [h]

2 ①

3 1. ② 2. ③

4 1. 타 2. 추

B Writing Practice

1 Combine each consonant and vowel to create a character.

	ㅏ (a)	ㅓ (eo)	ㅗ (o)	ㅜ (u)	ㅡ (eu)	ㅣ (i)	ㅐ (ae)	ㅔ (e)
ㅊ (ch)	차	처						
ㅋ (k)								
ㅌ (t)								
ㅍ (p)								
ㅎ (h)								

Practice reading and writing the words in Korean.

car / tea	차	차	cheese	치즈	치즈
coffee	커피	커피	nose	코	코
ostrich	타조	타조	fly	파리	파리
pepper	후추	후추	sun	해	해

4 Double Consonants (쌍자음)

We've learned a total of 14 consonants out of 19 so far. In this chapter, we will learn the remaining five consonants. These consonants are called "double consonant" because they are formed by combining two single consonants. Not all consonants can be doubled, and only ㄱ, ㄷ, ㅂ, ㅅ, and ㅈ can be paired, resulting in double consonants ㄲ, ㄸ, ㅃ, ㅆ, and ㅉ.

All double consonants produce tense sounds, which means you tighten your vocal cords while pronouncing them. When you tighten your vocal cords, your throat naturally becomes a bit restricted, causing less air to flow compared to aspirated consonants.

⊙ **TRACK 029**

Name	쌍기역 ssang*-gi-yeok
	*쌍(ssang) means "pair"
Sound	[g']
Memorization Tip	a tense ㄱ(g) sound

Pronunciation Guide

- With your vocal cords tightened, try producing the ㄱ(g) sound. This should create a doubled or stronger ㄱ sound.

Writing Practice

Name	쌍디귿 ssang-di-geut
Sound	[d']
Memorization Tip	a tense ㄷ (d) sound

Pronunciation Guide

· With your vocal cords tightened, try producing the ㄷ (d) sound. This should create a doubled or stronger ㄷ sound.

Writing Practice

Name	쌍비읍 ssang-bi-eup
Sound	[b']
Memorization Tip	a tense ㅂ (b) sound

Pronunciation Guide

· With your vocal cords tightened, try producing the ㅂ (b) sound. This should create a doubled or stronger ㅂ sound.

Writing Practice

Name	쌍시옷 ssang-si-ot
Sound	[s']
Memorization Tip	a stronger ㅅ(s) sound

Pronunciation Guide

- It is close to the English "s" sound but with more intensity and increased tension of your vocal cords.

Writing Practice

Name	쌍지읏 ssang-ji-eut
Sound	[j']
Memorization Tip	a tense ㅈ(j) sound

Pronunciation Guide

- With your vocal cords tightened, try producing the ㅈ(j) sound. This should create a doubled or stronger ㅈ sound.

Writing Practice

Let's compare the pronunciation of basic consonants, aspirated consonants, and double consonants.

TRACK 034

Basic	Aspirated	Double
1 ① 가	② 카	③ 까
2 ① 도	② 토	③ 또
3 ① 부	② 푸	③ 뿌
4 ① 재	② 채	③ 째
5 ① 시	② 씨	

1   Which one is a consonant that cannot make a double consonant?

①ㄱ   ②ㄷ   ③ㅁ   ④ㅈ

2   Listen to the audio and fill in each box with the character containing a double consonant.

▶ TRACK 035

① 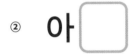 리

② 아

③ 그

④ 이 [ ] 시 개

⑤  개

3 Listen to the audio and select the one you hear.

▶ TRACK 036

1 ① 가드 ② 카드 ③ 까드

2 ① 도래 ② 토래 ③ 또래

3 ① 부자 ② 푸자 ③ 뿌자

4 ① 재소 ② 채소 ③ 째소

5 ① 아저시 ② 아저씨

ANSWER

1 ③

2 ① 꼬 ② 빠 ③ 때 ④ 쑤 ⑤ 찌

3 1. ② 2. ③ 3. ① 4. ② 5. ②

5 Diphthongs (이중 모음)

Well done! We've finished learning all the consonants in Hangeul.

Now, it's time to dive into the remaining vowels. We've already covered 8 out of the 21 vowels, leaving us with 13 more to explore. These 13 vowels are special, because they are formed by combining two single vowels, and we call them "compound vowels" or "diphthongs."

Among these, 6 produce a "y" sound, another 6 create a "w" sound, and the remaining one produces its own unique sound.

1. Diphthongs with a "y" sound

These diphthongs are characterized by their unique shape of two short lines, either vertical or horizontal.

ㅑ ㅕ ㅛ ㅠ ㅒ ㅖ

This visual pattern is a result of the ㅣ vowel, which, when combined with another vowel, produces the "y" sound and is commonly depicted as an extra short line within the character.

ㅣ [i]	+	ㅏ [a]	=	ㅑ [ya]
ㅣ [i]	+	ㅓ [eo]	=	ㅕ [yeo]
ㅣ [i]	+	ㅗ [o]	=	ㅛ [yo]
ㅣ [i]	+	ㅜ [u]	=	ㅠ [yu]
ㅣ [i]	+	ㅐ [ae]	=	ㅒ [yae]
ㅣ [i]	+	ㅔ [e]	=	ㅖ [ye]

Now let's take a close look at these six diphthongs one by one.

[ya]

Pronunciation Guide
It sounds close to "ya," as in the English word "yard," but with less elongation.

Writing Practice

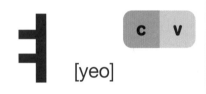

[yeo]

Pronunciation Guide
It sounds close to "yuh," as in the English word "yummy," but with less elongation.

Writing Practice

 [yo]

Pronunciation Guide

It sounds close to "yo," as in the English word "yo-yo," but with less elongation.

Writing Practice

 [yu]

Pronunciation Guide

It sounds close to the English word "you," but with less elongation.

Writing Practice

[yae]

Pronunciation Guide

It sounds close to "yae," as in the English word "yay," but with less elongation.

Writing Practice

[ye]

Pronunciation Guide

It sounds close to "ye," as in the English word "yes," but with less elongation.

▸ The difference between ㅐ and ㅖ is the same as how ㅐ and ㅔ differ. Your mouth is slightly more open when pronouncing ㅐ, and ㅖ is pronounced with slightly less effort.

These are very subtle differences that are hard to distinguish, especially at first. It is generally acceptable to pronounce them the same way.

Writing Practice

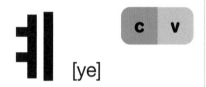

2. Diphthongs with a "w" sound

Diphthongs with a "w" sound are formed when the vowel ㅗ or ㅜ comes as the first vowel in the combination and blend with another vowel.

ㅗ [o] + ㅏ [a] = ㅘ [wa]

ㅜ [u] + ㅓ [eo] = ㅝ [wo]

ㅗ [o] + ㅐ [ae] = ㅙ [wae]

ㅜ [u] + ㅔ [e] = ㅞ [we]

ㅗ [o] + ㅣ [i] = ㅚ [oe]

ㅜ [u] + ㅣ [i] = ㅟ [wi]

Let's take a look at them one by one.

Each of these vowels is placed **below** and **next to** the consonant, creating a visual where the it embraces the consonant from below and around its side.

⊙ TRACK 043

ㅘ [wa]

Pronunciation Guide
It sounds close to "wa," as in the English word "what," but with less elongation.

Writing Practice

⊙ TRACK 044

ㅝ [wo]

Pronunciation Guide
It sounds close to "wo," as in the English word "water," but with less elongation.

Writing Practice

[wae]

Pronunciation Guide

It sounds close to "wae," as in the English word "where," but with less elongation.

Writing Practice

 [we]

Pronunciation Guide

It sounds close to "we," as in the English word "well," but with less elongation.

Writing Practice

 [oe]

Pronunciation Guide

It sounds close to "we," as in the English word "way," but with less elongation.

Writing Practice

ㅙ, ㅞ, and ㅚ
have subtle differences in mouth shape:

- ㅙ (wae)   The mouth is more open, and the lips are wider apart.

- ㅞ (we)   The mouth is moderately open, and the position of the lips is in the middle.

- ㅚ (oe)   The mouth is somewhat more closed, and the lips are either in the middle or slightly forward.

These are subtle differences that are hard to distinguish, especially at first. It's generally acceptable to pronounce them the same way.

⊙ TRACK 048

 [wi]

Pronunciation Guide
It sounds close to "wi," as in the English word "win," but with less elongation.

Writing Practice

3. A diphthong with a "ui" sound

The last diphthong is represented by the character ㅢ, and it makes a unique "ui" sound. This sound is formed by combining two vowel sounds, ㅡ(eu) and ㅣ(i).

$$\boxed{ㅡ}_{[eu]} + \boxed{ㅣ}_{[i]} = \boxed{ㅢ}_{[ui]}$$

The way ㅢ is pronounced is distinct and doesn't have a direct equivalent in English.

⊙ TRACK 049

[ui]

Pronunciation Guide

- It's a fast combination of ㅡ(eu) and ㅣ(i) sounds.

- For ㅡ(eu) : Gently stretch your lips sideways, open your lips a bit, and then make a sound. Do not let your teeth touch each other, and make sure that your front teeth are not fully covered by your lips.

- For ㅣ(i) : It's similar to the English "ee" in "see," but with less elongation.

- Try pronouncing these two sounds sequentially, but quickly.

Writing Practice

1 Match each vowel with the correct romanization.

1 ① ㅑ •　　　　　　　　• [yo]

　② ㅕ •　　　　　　　　• [ya]

　③ ㅛ •　　　　　　　　• [yeo]

　④ ㅠ •　　　　　　　　• [yu]

2 ① ㅘ •　　　　　　　　• [ui]

　② ㅝ •　　　　　　　　• [wo] (as in water)

　③ ㅟ •　　　　　　　　• [wi]

　④ ㅢ •　　　　　　　　• [wa] (as in what)

2 Select a vowel that sounds the same as ㅐ.

① ㅙ　　　　　② ㅚ　　　　　③ ㅔ　　　　　④ ㅖ

3 Select a vowel that sounds completely different from the rest.

① ㅙ　　　　　② ㅚ　　　　　③ ㅝ　　　　　④ ㅔ

4 Listen to the audio and select the one you hear.

⊙ TRACK 050

1　① 혜　　　② 휴　　　③ 회　　　④ 화

2　① 쥐　　　② 죄　　　③ 줘　　　④ 좌

3　① 야유　　② 여유　　③ 여우　　④ 우유

4　① 의사　　② 의자　　③ 야자　　④ 예사

5　① 야기　　② 얘기　　③ 위기　　④ 여기

5 Listen to the audio and select the correct vowel in the blank.

⊙ **TRACK 051**

1

 뻐

① ㅖ   ② ㅕ   ③ ㅑ   ④ ㅟ

2

 지

① ㅘ   ② ㅝ   ③ ㅙ   ④ ㅢ

ANSWER

1 1. ① [ya]   ② [yeo]   ③ [yo]   ④ [yu]
    2. ① [wa]   ② [wo]   ③ [wi]   ④ [ui]

2 ④

3 ③

4 1. ④   2. ①   3. ②   4. ①   5. ②

5 1. ①   2. ③

6 | Final Consonants / Batchim(받침)

> Korean final consonants are commonly referred to as "batchim." Both terms are used interchangeably throughout this book.

Do you remember that each consonant had a name? You might have noticed that each name begins with the sound of the consonant itself. Another interesting fact is that the name of each consonant ends with the sound it makes as a final consonant. So, just by looking at the name of a consonant, you will know how it sounds not only as a consonant but also as a final consonant.

There are seven sounds that can be made by final consonants in Korean. You might wonder why there are far fewer sounds than the number of consonants. This is because there are many final consonants that produce the same sounds. Korean final consonants are typically pronounced without a distinct consonant sound at the very end, which naturally leads to some of them having identical sounds. You will gain a better understanding of this through explanations and audio examples.

The final consonants that share the same sounds are grouped together in this chapter, which will help you learn them group by group.

⊙ **TRACK 052**

ㄱ 역 / 각 / 백
yeok gak baek

The name of ㄱ is 기역, with the last character 역 romanized as "yeok".
gi-yeok
This makes it easy to remember that the final consonant ㄱ is pronounced like the
English "k" sound when it's at the end of a word.

However, it's not exactly the same as the final "k" sound in English. For example,
when pronouncing the English words "back" or "sock," the "k" consonant sound is
clearly audible at the very end. But when pronouncing the Korean word 역[yeok], your
pronunciation stops right before producing the distinct "k" sound.

You can think of it as pronouncing only two-thirds of the final "k" sound in English.

ㅋ 윽 / 억
euk eok

The name of ㅋ is 키읔, with the last character 읔 romanized as "euk."
ki-euk
This makes it easy to remember that the final consonant ㅋ is pronounced like the
English "k" sound when it's at the end of a word. Its pronunciation is the same as the
final consonant ㄱ; it does not produce a distinct consonant sound at the end.

However, when the next character starts with the consonant ㅇ, the final consonants
ㄱ and ㅋ will combine with the vowel sound of the following character, creating
the sound of an initial consonant and resulting in different sounds respectively.

For example,
억에 is pronounced [어게], while 엌에 is pronounced [어케].
But when 억[eok] and 엌[eok] are independent characters, they have the same sound.

This will be covered again in the chapter on consonant assimilation.

2. The final "n" sound – ㄴ

TRACK 053

ㄴ
은 / 난 / 괜
eun nan gwaen

The name of ㄴ is 니은, with the last character 은 romanized as "eun."
ni-eun
This makes it easy to remember that the final consonant ㄴ is pronounced like the English "n" sound when it's at the end of a word.

However, it's not exactly the same as the final "n" sound in English. For example, when pronouncing the English words "on" or "win," the "n" consonant sound is clearly audible at the very end. But when pronouncing the Korean word 은[eun], your pronunciation stops right before producing distinct "n" sound.

You can think of it as pronouncing only two-thirds of the final "n" sound in English.

3. The final "t" sound – ㄷ, ㅅ, ㅈ, ㅊ, ㅌ, ㅎ

TRACK 054

ㄷ
귿 / 닫 / 곧
geut dat got

The name of ㄷ is 디귿, with the last character 귿 romanized as "geut."
di-geut
This makes it easy to remember that the final consonant ㄷ is pronounced like the English "t" sound when it's at the end of a word.

However, it's not exactly the same as the final "t" sound in English. For example, when pronouncing the English words "bat" or "cat," the "t" consonant sound is clearly audible at the very end. But when pronouncing the Korean word 귿[geut], your pronunciation stops right before producing the distinct "t" sound.

You can think of it as pronouncing only two-thirds of the final "t" sound in English.

ㅅ 옷 / 셋 / 곳
  ot   set   got

The name of ㅅ is 시옷, with the last character 옷 romanized as "ot."
si-ot
This makes it easy to remember that the final consonant ㅅ is pronounced like the English "t" sound when it's at the end of a word.

Its pronunciation is the same as the batchim ㄷ;

it does not produce a distinct consonant sound at the end.

ㅈ 읒 / 잦 / 낮
  eut   jat   nat

The name of ㅈ is 지읒, with the last character 읒 romanized as "eut."
ji-eut
This makes it easy to remember that the final consonant ㅈ is pronounced like the English "t" sound when it's at the end of a word.

Its pronunciation is the same as the batchim ㄷ;

it does not produce a distinct consonant sound at the end.

ㅊ 읓 / 낯
  eut   nat

The name of ㅊ is 치읓, with the last character 읓 romanized as "eut."
chi-eut
This makes it easy to remember that the final consonant ㅊ is pronounced like the English "t" sound when it's at the end of a word.

Its pronunciation is the same as the batchim ㄷ;

it does not produce a distinct consonant sound at the end.

The name of ㅌ is 티읕, with the last character 읕 romanized as "eut."

This makes it easy to remember that the final consonant ㅌ is pronounced like the English "t" sound when it's at the end of a word.

Its pronunciation is the same as the batchim ㄷ;

it does not produce a distinct consonant sound at the end.

The name of ㅎ is 히읗, with the last character 읗 romanized as "eut."

This makes it easy to remember that the final consonant ㅎ is pronounced like the English "t" sound when it's at the end of a word.

Its pronunciation is the same as the batchim ㄷ;

it does not produce a distinct consonant sound at the end.

> ▸ Tongue Tip : When making the final "t" sound in English, your tongue touches the back
> of your front teeth before lifting off. But for Korean batchims ㄷ, ㅅ, ㅈ, ㅊ,
> ㅌ, and ㅎ, keep your tongue there without lifting off.

These six final consonants are all pronounced the same when they appear in a single character. However, the pronunciation rules can vary depending on the following consonant in the next character. This will be covered in more detail in the chapter on consonant assimilation.

4. The final "l" sound – ㄹ

⊙ TRACK 055

ㄹ   을 / 릴 / 물
       eul   lil   mul

The name of ㄹ is 리을, with the last character 을 romanized as "eul."
li-eul

This makes it easy to remember that the final consonant ㄹ is pronounced like

the English "l" sound when it's at the end of a word.

However, it's not exactly the same as the final "l" sound in English. For example, when

pronouncing the English words "pal" or "soil," the "l" consonant sound is

more distinct and elongated. But when pronouncing the Korean word 을[eul],

your pronunciation stops right before elongating the "l" sound.

You can think of it as pronouncing only two-thirds of the final "l" sound in English.

▸ **Tongue Tip** : Leave your tongue at the roof of your mouth and don't take it off.

5. The final "m" sound – ㅁ

⊙ TRACK 056

ㅁ   음 / 몸 / 님
       eum mom   nim

The name of ㅁ is 미음, with the last character 음 romanized as "eum."
mi-eum

This makes it easy to remember that the final consonant ㅁ is pronounced like

the English "m" sound when it's at the end of a word.

▸ **Mouth Tip** : When pronouncing the batchims ㅁ, ㅂ, and ㅍ, close your lips as soon as

they touch and don't let them pop open.

However, it's not exactly the same as the final "m" sound in English. For example, when pronouncing the English words "gym" or "sum," the "m" consonant sound is clearly audible at the very end. But when pronouncing the Korean word 음[eum], your pronunciation stops right before producing the distinct "m" sound.

You can think of it as pronouncing only two-thirds of the final "m" sound in English.

6. The final "p" sound – ㅂ, ㅍ

⊙ TRACK 057

ㅂ   읍 / 밥 / 십
       eup   bap   sip

The name of ㅂ is 비읍, with the last character 읍 romanized as "eup."
     bi-eup
This makes it easy to remember that the final consonant ㅂ is pronounced like the English "p" sound when it's at the end of a word.

However, it's not exactly the same as the final "p" sound in English. For example, when pronouncing the English words "map" or "soup," the "p" consonant sound is clearly audible at the very end. But when pronouncing the Korean word 읍[eup], your pronunciation stops right before producing the distinct "p" sound.

You can think of it as pronouncing only two-thirds of the final "p" sound in English.

음 / 싶
eup   sip

The name of ㅍ is 피읖, and the last character 읖 is romanized as "eup."
pi-eup

This makes it easy to remember that the final consonant ㅍ is pronounced like the English "p" sound when it's at the end of a word.

Its pronunciation is the same as the batchim ㅂ;
it does not produce a distinct consonant sound at the end.

7. The final "ng" sound – ㅇ

⊙ TRACK 058

응 / 녕 / 송
eung   nyeong   song

The name of ㅇ is 이응, with the last character 응 romanized as "eung."
i-eung

This makes it easy to remember the final consonant ㅇ is pronounced like the English "ng" sound when it's at the end of a word, like "song" or "ring" in English.

However, it's not exactly the same as the final "ng" sound in English.
For example, when pronouncing the English words "song" or "ring," the "ng" sound is elongated, and some even pronounce it with the "g" consonant sound at the very end. But when pronouncing the Korean word 응[eung], your pronunciation doesn't stretch out and stops right before producing the distinct "g" sound.

You can think of it as pronouncing only two-thirds of the final "ng" sound in English.

1 Select one syllable that sounds <u>different</u> from the other three.

① 억   ② 얻   ③ 엇   ④ 엳

2 Select one syllable that sounds that same as 압.

① 앚   ② 앝   ③ 앞   ④ 앟

3 Among the following six characters, which one (or ones) produces the same sound as 억 and 얻? Write down the corresponding characters next to each one.

엇 엊 엋 억 얻 엃

억 = _____

얻 = _____

4 Select the correct romanization for each syllable.

1 강   ① [ga]   ② [gan]   ③ [gang]   ④ [gam]

2 벽   ① [byeong] ② [byeok]   ③ [byeon]   ④ [byeot]

3 풀   ① [pul]   ② [pun]   ③ [pum]   ④ [pung]

4 섬   ① [seom]   ② [seop]   ③ [seot]   ④ [seong]

5 집   ① [jin]   ② [jit]   ③ [jim]   ④ [jip]

5 Listen to the aduio and select the right final consonant for each syllable.

⊙ TRACK 059

1

① ㅁ ② ㄹ ③ ㄴ ④ ㅅ

2

① ㄴ ② ㄹ ③ ㅂ ④ ㄷ

3

① ㄱ ② ㅅ ③ ㄴ ④ ㅁ

ANSWER

1 ①

2 ③

3 억 = 억, 얻 = 엇, 엊, 얼, 얻, 얼

4 1. ③ 2. ② 3. ① 4. ① 5. ④

5 1. ③ 2. ④ 3. ④

7 Compound Final Consonants (겹받침)

Compound final consonants, as the name suggests, are two consonants that appear in the final position of a character. Unlike initial consonants, you can combine two consonants for final consonants. However, not all combinations are accepted and only 13 combinations are used. They must be used exactly as specified, and the order of the two consonants cannot be changed.

Among the 13 compound final consonants, 2 are double consonants, which consist of the same consonant repeated, and the other 11 are combinations of different consonants.

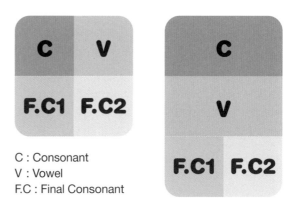

C : Consonant
V : Vowel
F.C : Final Consonant

Let's start with the double consonants.

1. Double Consonants

⊙ TRACK 060

We've learned five double consonants in Hangeul, but only two of them can be used as a final consonant.

Those two are ㄲ (쌍기역, double gi-yeok) and ㅆ (쌍시옷, double si-ot).
ssang-gi-yeok   ssang-si-ot

❶

It is pronounced the same as the final consonant ㄱ.

❷

It is pronounced the same as the final consonant ㅅ.

However, as we'll explore further in the chapter on consonant assimilation, when the next character starts with the consonant ㅇ, each final consonant combines with the vowel sound of the following character, creating the sound of an initial consonant and resulting in different sounds respectively.

For example,

박에 is pronounced [바게], and

밖에 is pronounced [바께].

웃어 is pronounced [우서], and

왔어 is pronounced [와써].

But when each of them appears in an individual character, they have the same sound.

2. Combinations of Two Different Consonants

⊙ TRACK 061

Now, we will study the final consonants that are formed by combining two different consonants. There are a total of 11 combinations. 8 of these final consonants follow the pronunciation of the first consonant, while the other 3 follow that of the second consonant.

The colored consonant in each combination indicates the pronunciation it follows.

➊

It is pronounced as the final consonant ㄱ.

When it's followed by the consonant ㅇ in the next character, then ㄱ remains in the previous character and ㅅ makes an initial consonant sound by combining with the vowel sound of the following character.

* The pronunciation is written with ㅆ instead of ㅅ, because the consonant ㅅ produces a stronger sound when combined with the batchim ㄱ. This will be explored further in the chapter on consonant assimilation.

➋

It is pronounced as the final consonant ㄴ.

앉 [안] 엱 [언]
an eon

When it's followed by the consonant ㅇ in the next character, then ㄴ remains in the previous character and ㅈ makes an initial consonant sound by combining with the vowel sound of the following character.

앉 아 [안자] 엱 어 [언저]
an-ja eon-jeo

❸

It is pronounced as the final consonant ㄴ.

않 [안] 많 [만]
an man

When it's followed by the consonant ㅇ in the next character, then ㅎ remains silent and ㄴ makes an initial consonant sound by combining with the vowel sound of the following character.

않 아 [아나] 많 아 [마나]
a-na ma-na

When it's followed by the consonants ㄱ, ㄷ, and ㅈ in the next character, then ㅎ merges with them and creates aspirated sounds : ㅋ, ㅌ, and ㅊ respectively.

▶ This will be covered again in the chapter on consonant assimilation.

않 고 [안코] 않 다 [안타] 많 지 [만치]
an-ko an-ta man-chi

❹

It is pronounced as the final consonant ㄱ.

닭 [닥]
dak

읽 [익]
ik

When it's followed by the consonant ㅇ in the next character, then ㄹ remains in the previous character and ㄱ makes an initial consonant sound by combining with the vowel sound of the following character.

읽 어 [일거]
il-geo

닭 이 [달기]
dal-gi

❺

It is pronounced as the final consonant ㅁ.

삶 [삼]
sam

젊 [점]
jeom

When it's followed by the consonant ㅇ in the next character, then ㄹ remains in the previous character and ㅁ makes an initial consonant sound by combining with the vowel sound of the following character.

삶 이 [살미]
sal-mi

젊 음 [절믐]
jeol-meum

❻

It is pronounced as the final consonant ㄹ.

 **[여덜]**
yeo-deol

When it's followed by the consonant ㅇ in the next character, then ㄹ remains in the previous character and ㅂ makes an initial consonant sound by combining with the vowel sound of the following character.

 **[발바]**
bal-ba

 **[널버]**
neol-beo

❼

It is pronounced as the final consonant ㄹ.
There are very few Korean words spelled with this final consonant.

❽

It is pronounced as the final consonant ㄹ.

 [할]
hal

 [훌]
hul

When it's followed by the consonant ㅇ in the next character, then ㄹ remains in the previous character and ㅌ makes an initial consonant sound by combining with the vowel sound of the following character.

핥 아 [할타]
hal-ta

훑 어 [훌터]
hul-teo

❾

It is pronounced as the final consonant ㅍ.

읊 [읖]
eup

When it's followed by the consonant ㅇ in the next character, then ㄹ remains in the previous character and ㅍ makes an initial consonant sound by combining with the vowel sound of the following character.

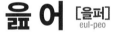

읊 어 [을퍼]
eul-peo

❿

It is pronoucned as the final consonant ㄹ.

싫 [실]
sil

잃 [일]
il

When it's followed by the consonant ㅇ in the next character, then ㅎ remains silent and ㄹ makes an initial consonant sound by combining with the vowel sound of the following character.

 싫 어 [시러]
si-leo

 잃 어 [이러]
i-leo

When it's followed by the consonants ㄱ, ㄷ, and ㅈ in the next character, then ㅎ merges with them and creates aspirated sounds : ㅋ, ㅌ, and ㅊ respectively.

▶This will be covered again in the chapter on consonant assimilation.

싫 고 [실코]
sil-ko

싫 다 [실타]
sil-ta

잃 지 [일치]
il-chi

⑪

It is pronoucned as the final consonant ㅂ.

없 [업]
eop

값 [갑]
gap

When it's followed by the consonant ㅇ in the next character, then ㅂ remains in the previous character and ㅅ makes an initial consonant sound by combining with the vowel sound of the following character.

없 어 [업써]
eop-sseo

값 이 [갑씨]*
gap-ssi

* The pronunciation is written with ㅆ instead of ㅅ, because the consonant ㅅ produces a stronger sound when combined with the batchim ㅂ. This will be explored further in the chapter on consonant assimilation.

1 Select <u>two</u> double consonants that can be used as a 받침(final consonant).
batchim

① ㄲ   ② ㄸ   ③ ㅃ   ④ ㅆ   ⑤ ㅉ

2 Select the correct pronunciation of each word.

1   넋   ① [넉]   ② [넛]

2   값   ① [갑]   ② [갓]

3   닭   ① [달]   ② [닥]

4   삶   ① [살]   ② [삼]

3 Select the correct pronunciation of 읽어요.

① [이러요]   ② [이거요]   ③ [일거요]

4 Select the correct pronunciation of 밟아요.

① [바라요]   ② [발바요]   ③ [바바요]

5 Select the correct pronunciation of 싫어요.

① [시러요]   ② [실러요]   ③ [실허요]

6 Select the correct pronunciation of 많게.

① [만게]   ② [마케]   ③ [만케]

ANSWER

1   ①, ④   2   1. ①   2. ①   3. ②   4. ②

3   ③   4   ②

5   ①   6   ③

8 Consonant Assimilation (자음 동화)

You have learned all the Korean consonants, vowels, and final consonants. Now, you can read and write anything in Korean!

The final topic to explore in Hangeul is consonant assimilation. It's all about how sounds change when the final consonant of one character meets the initial consonant of the next. For example, in the previous chapter, it was briefly mentioned how the final consonant ㅎ, when it meets ㄱ, ㄷ, and ㅈ, produces the sounds ㅋ, ㅌ, and ㅊ, respectively. This is part of the consonant assimilation rules.

Despite being labeled as "rules," it would be more helpful to approach it as a natural phonetic phenomenon for Korean speakers.

You can still read Korean even if you don't know consonant assimilation rules. However, understanding these rules not only makes your pronunciation smoother and more native-like, but it also greatly improves your ability to listen and speak Korean, because listening and speaking are closely related to pronunciation. Last but not least, it also helps you remember spellings more accurately when learning new words.

Consonant assimilation rules are quite diverse, and trying to learn all of them from the very beginning can be overwhelming. Moreover, some combinations are pronounced irregularly on a word-by-word basis rather than following consistent rules. They are not necessarily influenced by consonant assimilation but rather represent the most natural and comfortable pronunciation for native speakers.

As a beginner, it's not necessary to learn all of these variations. It's more effective to start with the most common rules, which are conveniently compiled in this chapter.

Now, let's explore further into some of the most common consonant assimilation rules.

Before You Learn

1. The order of the final consonants will be presented in the same way as provided in the final consonant chapter.

2. Any missing combinations are due to their rarity or complexity.

3. This chapter focuses on pronunciation guidance, so there's no need to worry about memorizing the meanings of each example word provided.

1. The final "k" sound – ㄱ, ㅋ

When the final "k" sound is combined with basic consonants ㄱ, ㄷ, ㅅ, ㅂ, and ㅈ, each of these consonants creates a stronger sound, resulting in a double consonant sound.

(The same phenomenon happens when these basic consonants follow batchims that end with the final "t" and "p" sound. It will be revisited later in this chapter.)

⊙ **TRACK 062**

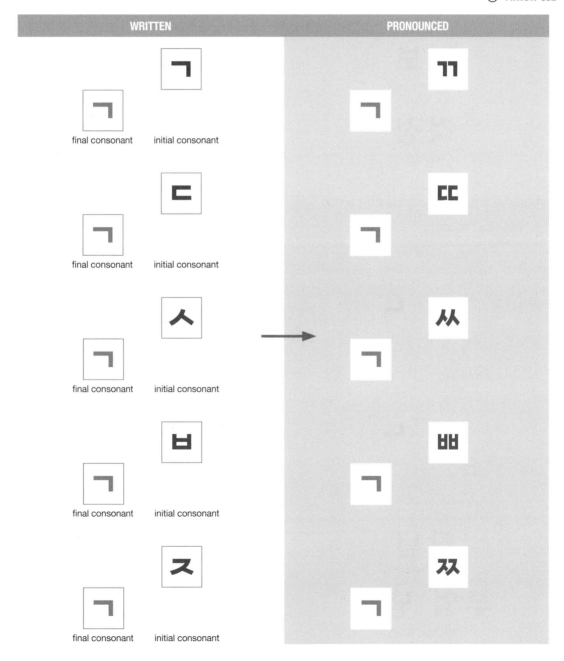

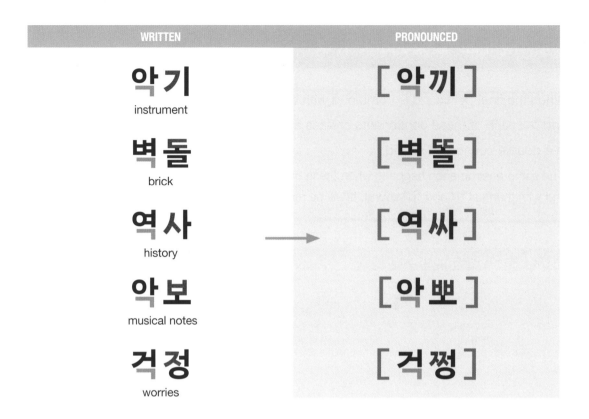

WRITTEN	PRONOUNCED
악기 instrument	[악끼]
벽돌 brick	[벽똘]
역사 history	[역싸]
악보 musical notes	[악뽀]
걱정 worries	[걱쩡]

When the final "k" sound is combined with the consonants ㄴ, ㄹ and ㅁ, it softens to the final "ng" sound.

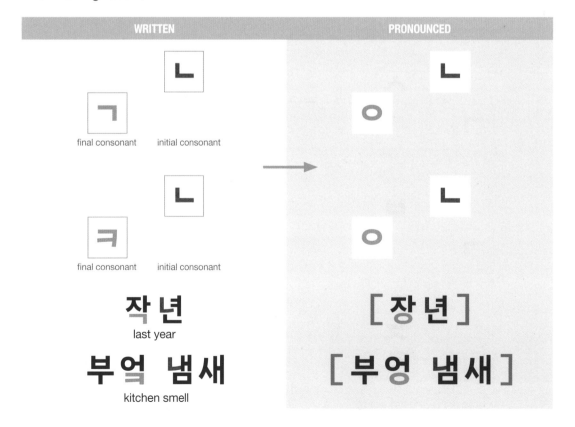

WRITTEN	PRONOUNCED
작년 last year	[장년]
부엌 냄새 kitchen smell	[부엉 냄새]

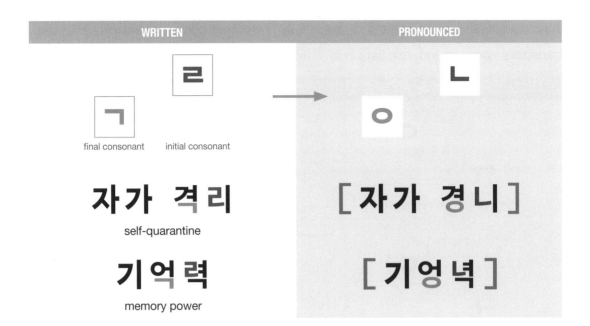

WRITTEN	PRONOUNCED
자가 격리 self-quarantine	[자가 경니]
기억력 memory power	[기엉녁]

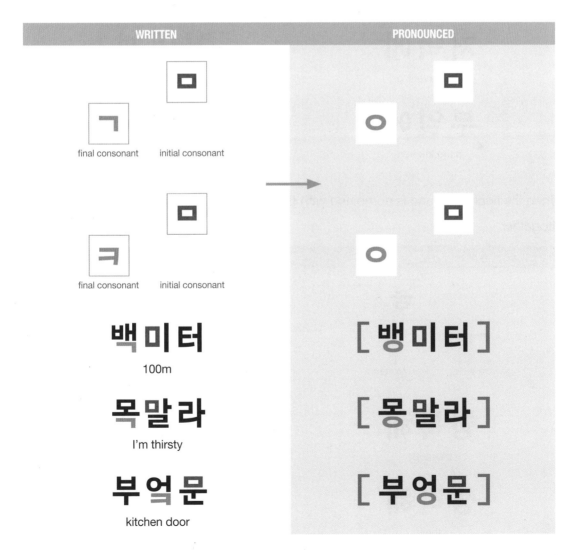

WRITTEN	PRONOUNCED
백미터 100m	[뱅미터]
목말라 I'm thirsty	[몽말라]
부엌문 kitchen door	[부엉문]

final consonant initial consonant

When the following consonant is ㅇ, each final consonant combines with the following character's vowel sound, resulting in an initial consonant sound.

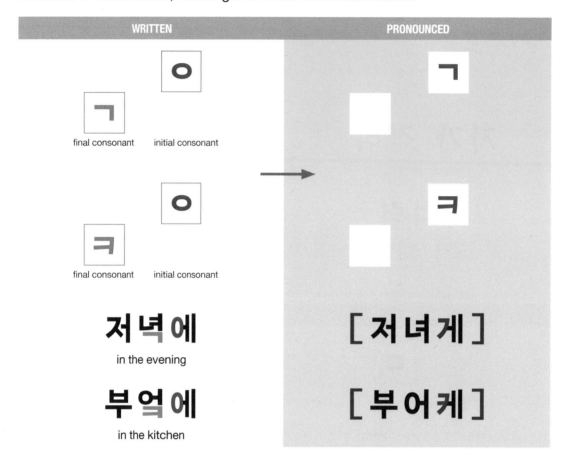

저녁에
in the evening

부엌에
in the kitchen

[저녀게]

[부어케]

When the final "k" sound is combined with the consonant ㅎ, it results in the ㅋ sound altogether.

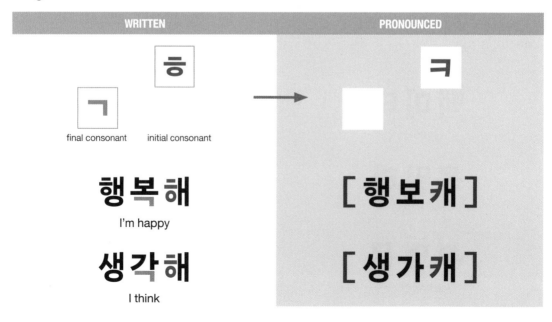

행복해
I'm happy

생각해
I think

[행보캐]

[생가캐]

2. The final "n" sound - ㄴ

When the final "n" sound is combined with the consonant ㄹ, it becomes the final "l" sound. This may not seem intuitive to some learners, but it's the most natural pronunciation for native speakers.

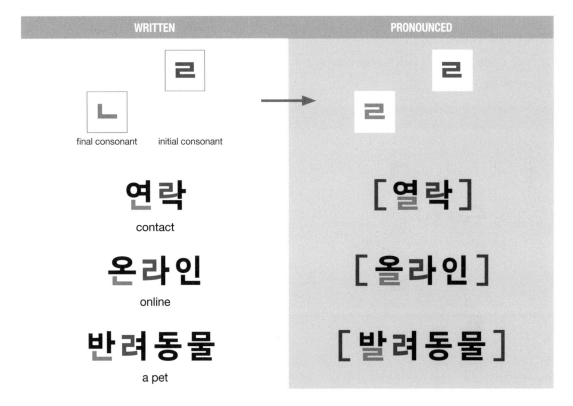

When the following consonant is ㅇ, each final consonant combines with the following character's vowel sound, resulting in an initial consonant sound.

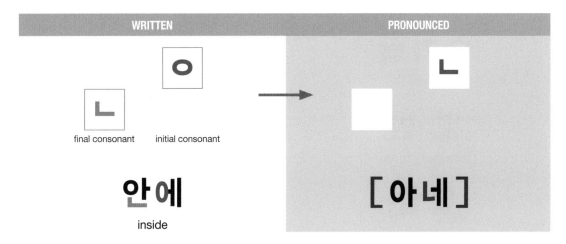

3. The final "t" sound – ㄷ, ㅅ, ㅈ, ㅊ, ㅌ, ㅎ

⊙ TRACK 064

❶ The final consonants ㄷ, ㅅ, ㅈ, ㅊ, ㅌ

When the final "t" sound is combined with basic consonants ㄱ, ㄷ, ㅅ, ㅂ, and ㅈ, each of these consonants creates a stronger sound, resulting in a double consonant sound.

(This rule does not apply to the final consonant ㅎ. More about this will be covered in the section on ㅎ.)

WRITTEN	PRONOUNCED

숟가락
spoon

[숟까락]

몇 번
how many times

[면 뻔]

밑줄
underline

[믿쭐]

When the final "t" sound is combined with the consonants ㄴ and ㅁ, it softens to the final "n" sound.

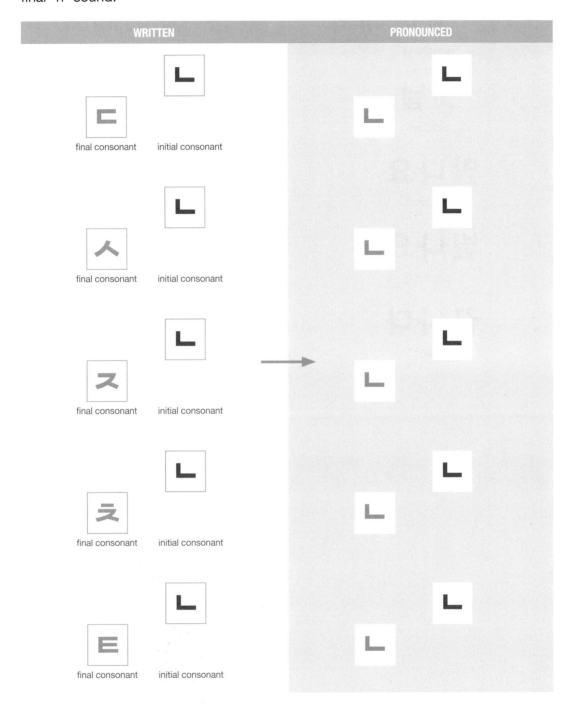

WRITTEN	PRONOUNCED

WRITTEN	PRONOUNCED
걷는 중이에요 is walking	[건는 중이에요]
옛날 old days	[옌날]
맞나요 Is it correct?	[만나요]
빛나요 is shining	[빈나요]
끝나다 to end	[끈나다]

걷는 중이에요.

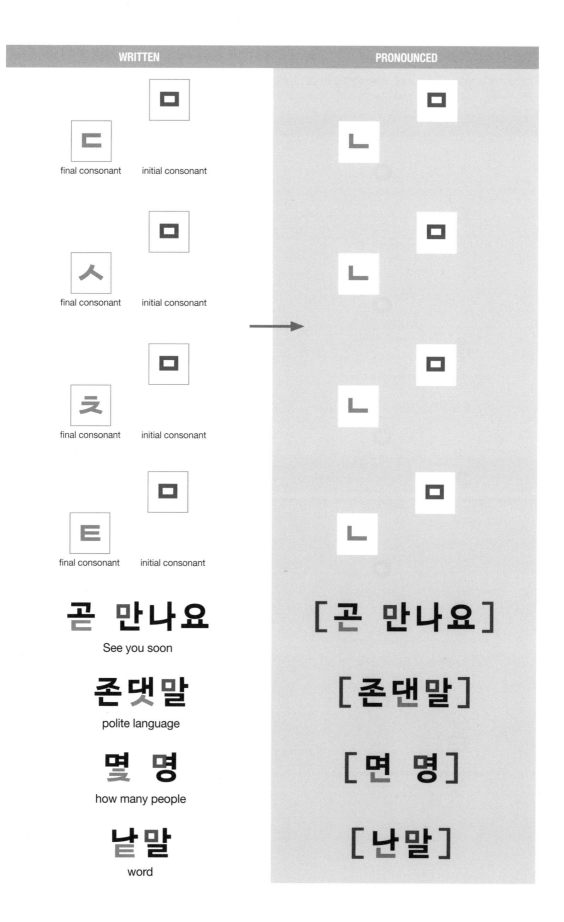

ㄷ final consonant　ㅁ initial consonant → ㄴ ㅁ

ㅅ final consonant　ㅁ initial consonant → ㄴ ㅁ

ㅊ final consonant　ㅁ initial consonant → ㄴ ㅁ

ㅌ final consonant　ㅁ initial consonant → ㄴ ㅁ

곧 만나요
See you soon
[곤 만나요]

존댓말
polite language
[존댄말]

몇 명
how many people
[면 명]

낱말
word
[난말]

When the following consonant is ㅇ, each final consonant combines with the following character's vowel sound, resulting in an initial consonant sound.

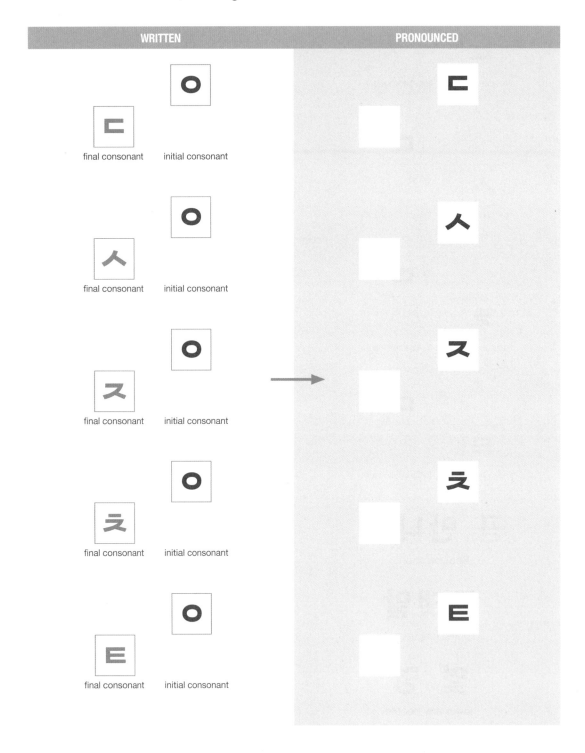

WRITTEN	PRONOUNCED
ㄷ final consonant · ㅇ initial consonant	ㄷ
ㅅ final consonant · ㅇ initial consonant	ㅅ
ㅈ final consonant · ㅇ initial consonant	ㅈ
ㅊ final consonant · ㅇ initial consonant	ㅊ
ㅌ final consonant · ㅇ initial consonant	ㅌ

WRITTEN	PRONOUNCED
믿어 I believe	**[미더]**
옷이 clothes + subject marker	**[오시]**
낮에 at day time	**[나제]**
빛이 light + subject marker	**[비치]**
밭에 in the field	**[바테]**

* Occasionally, some words within these combinations follow different pronunciation rules. For example, the word 같이 is pronounced as 가치, not 가티. As mentioned, such irregular patterns are based on what native speakers find most natural for different words. Whenever you come across such words during your studies, it's often more effective to simply accept and memorize pronunciation as native speakers say it, rather trying to find logical explanations.

When the batchim ㅅ is combined with the ㅎ consonant, it altogether produces the ㅌ sound. When the batchim ㅈ is combined with the ㅎ consonant, it altogether produces the ㅊ sound.

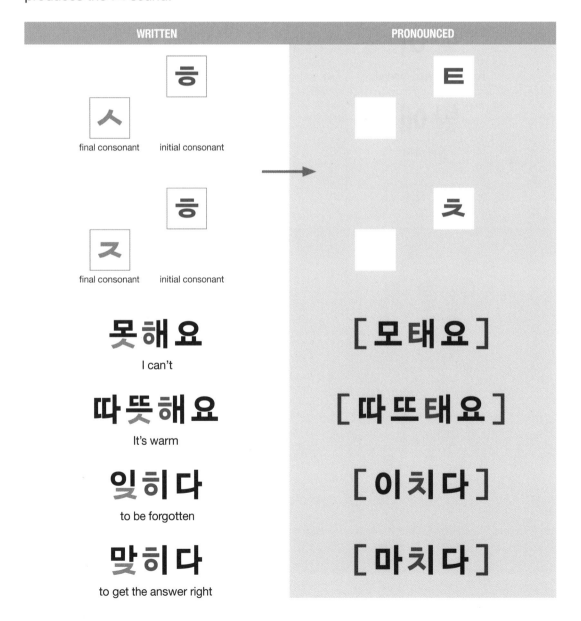

WRITTEN	PRONOUNCED

못해요
I can't

[모태요]

따뜻해요
It's warm

[따뜨태요]

잊히다
to be forgotten

[이치다]

맞히다
to get the answer right

[마치다]

❷ The final consonant ㅎ

When the batchim ㅎ is combined with the consonant ㄱ, ㄷ, and ㅈ,
it altogether produces ㅋ, ㅌ and ㅊ sounds respectively.

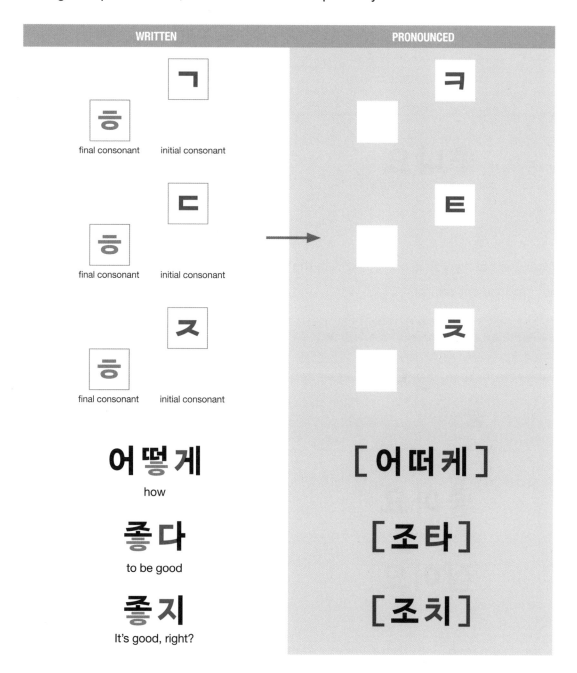

WRITTEN	PRONOUNCED
ㄱ ㅎ final consonant / initial consonant	ㅋ
ㄷ ㅎ final consonant / initial consonant	ㅌ
ㅈ ㅎ final consonant / initial consonant	ㅊ
어떻게 how	[어떠케]
좋다 to be good	[조타]
좋지 It's good, right?	[조치]

When the final "t" sound is combined with the consonant ㄴ, it softens to the final "n" sound.

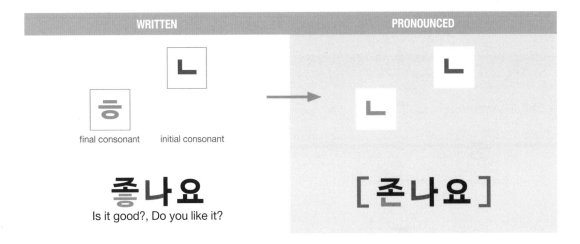

When the batchim ㅎ is combined with the consonant ㅇ, it remains silent and does not produce any sound.

4. The final "l" sound – ㄹ

▶ TRACK 065

When the final "l" sound is combined with the consonant ㄴ,
it changes the ㄴ sound to the ㄹ sound. This may not seem intuitive
to some learners, but it's the most natural pronunciation
for native speakers.

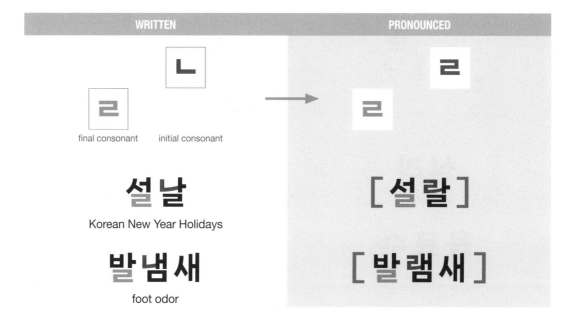

WRITTEN	PRONOUNCED

ㄹ (final consonant) ㄴ (initial consonant) → ㄹ ㄹ

설날
Korean New Year Holidays

[설랄]

발냄새
foot odor

[발램새]

5. The final "m" sound – ㅁ

⊙ TRACK 066

When the final "m" sound is combined with the consonant ㄹ, it changes the ㄹ sound to the ㄴ sound. This may not seem intuitive to some learners, but it's the most natural pronunciation for native speakers.

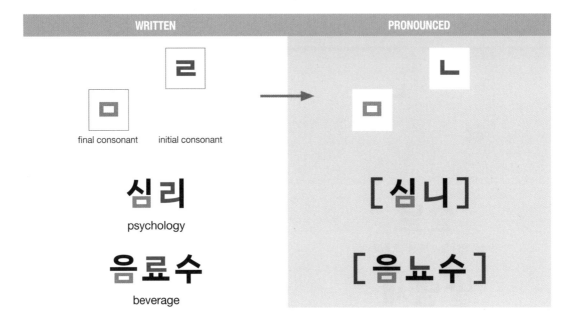

심리
psychology

[심니]

음료수
beverage

[음뇨수]

6. The final "p" sound – ㅂ, ㅍ

⊙ TRACK 067

When the final "p" sound is combined with basic consonants ㄱ, ㄷ, ㅅ, ㅂ, and ㅈ, each of these consonants creates a stronger sound, resulting in a double consonant sound.

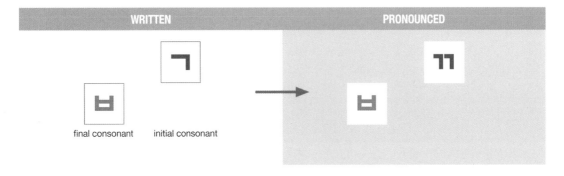

WRITTEN	PRONOUNCED

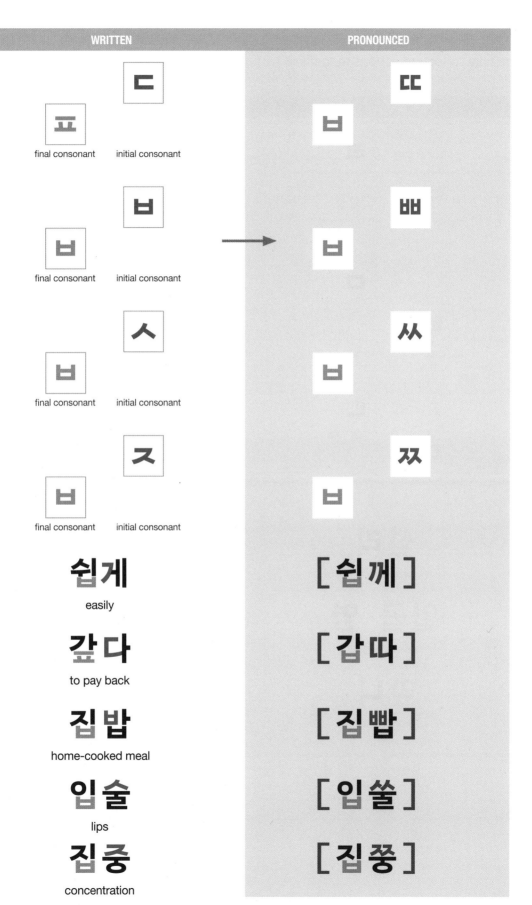

ㄷ

ㅍ
final consonant · initial consonant

→ ㄸ
ㅂ

ㅂ
ㅂ
final consonant · initial consonant

ㅃ
ㅂ

ㅅ
ㅂ
final consonant · initial consonant

ㅆ
ㅂ

ㅈ
ㅂ
final consonant · initial consonant

ㅉ
ㅂ

쉽게
easily

[쉽께]

갚다
to pay back

[갑따]

집밥
home-cooked meal

[집빱]

입술
lips

[입쑬]

집중
concentration

[집쭝]

When the final "p" sound is combined with the consonants ㄴ, ㄹ and ㅁ, the final "p" sound softens to the final "m" sound.

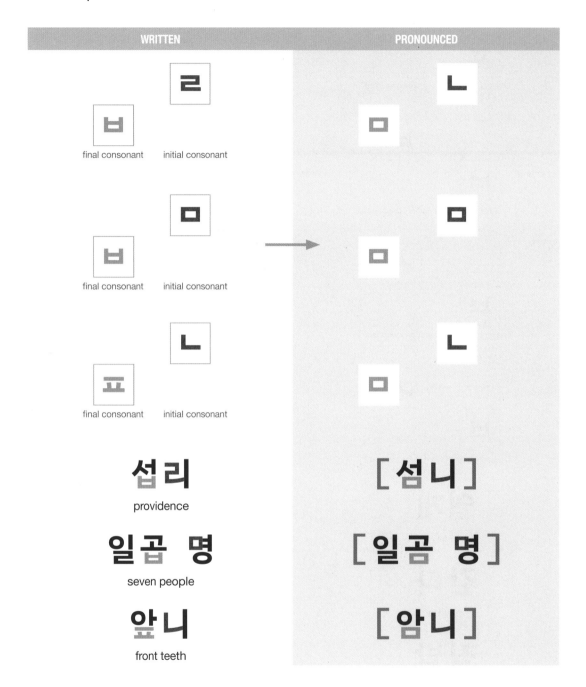

WRITTEN	PRONOUNCED

섭리
providence

[섬니]

일곱 명
seven people

[일곰 명]

앞니
front teeth

[암니]

When the following consonant is ㅇ, each final consonant combines with the following character's vowel sound, resulting in an initial consonant sound.

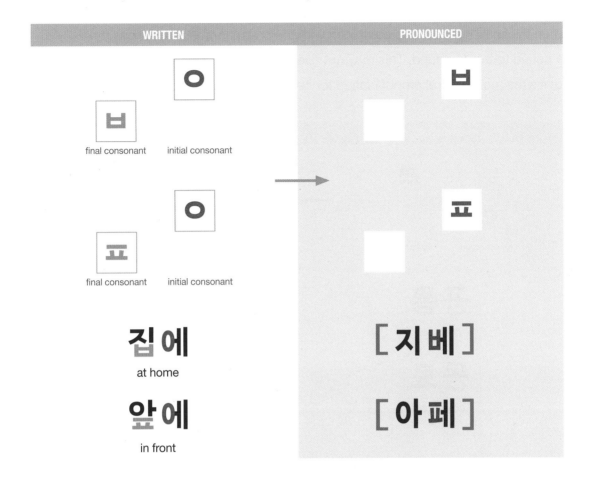

집에
at home

[지베]

앞에
in front

[아페]

When the final "p" sound is combined with the consonant ㅎ, it altogether produces the ㅍ sound.

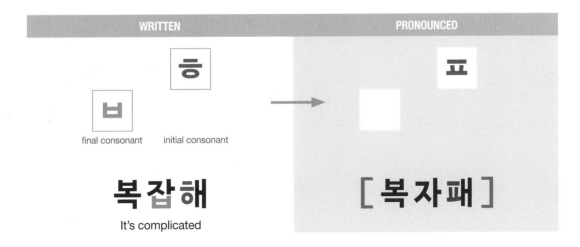

복잡해
It's complicated

[복자패]

7. The final "ng" sound – ㅇ

⊙ **TRACK 068**

When the final "ng" sound is combined with the consonant ㄹ, it changes the
ㄹ sound to the ㄴ sound. This may not seem intuitive to some learners,
but it's the most natural pronunciation for native speakers.

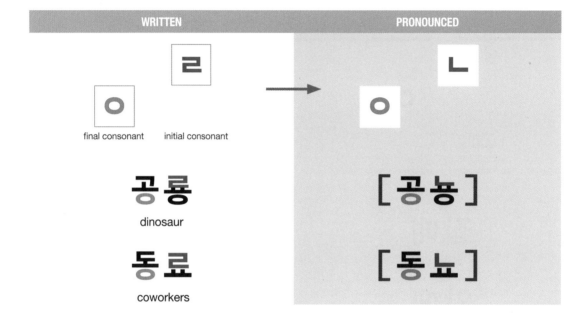

WRITTEN	PRONOUNCED

공룡
dinosaur

[공뇽]

동료
coworkers

[동뇨]

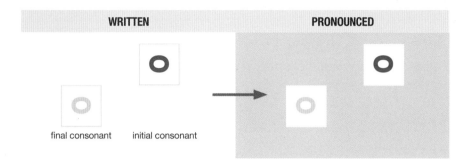

WRITTEN	PRONOUNCED

final consonant   initial consonant

영어 [영어] : English
　　영거 (X)

고양이 [고양이] : cat
　　고양기 (X)

This combination doesn't involve any assimilation, but learners often make the mistake of mispronouncing words with this combination; they often make the "g" sound because of how the batchim ㅇ is romanized as "ng."

For example, words like **영어** and **고양이** are commonly mispronounced as **영거** [yeong-geo] and **고양기** [go-yang-gi]. As we learned in the chapter on final consonants, the batchim ㅇ is romanized as "ng" because it's the closest match, but it doesn't contain a distinct "g" sound. The accurate pronunciations for each word are **영어** [yeong-eo] and **고양이** [go-yang-i]. The "g" sound should not be added to the following vowels 어[eo] and 이[i] .

1 Listen to the audio and fill in each box with the correct <u>consonant</u>.

⏵ TRACK 069

①

②

③

④

⑤

2 Listen to the audio and fill in each box with the correct <u>vowel</u>.

⏵ TRACK 070

①

②

③

④

⑤

3 Listen to the audio and fill in each box with the correct <u>final consonant</u>.

▶ TRACK 071

① 보 ☐

② 하 구

③ 겨 차

④ 지 아

4 Listen to the audio and fill in each box with the correct <u>double consonant</u>.

▶ TRACK 072

① ☐ㅌ

② ☐ㅏ

③ ☐ㅇ

④ ☐ㅣ

⑤ ☐ㅐ

5 Listen to the audio and write the word you hear.

▶ TRACK 073

①

②

③

④

⑤

6 Select one syllable that has a different sound from the rest.

① 겁   ② 겂   ③ 겉

7 Select one syllable that has a different sound from 맛.

① 맡   ② 맏   ③ 맞   ④ 막

8 Listen to the audio and select the word you hear.

⊙ **TRACK 074**

1 ① 의미 ② 와미 ③ 외미 ④ 위미

2 ① 가웨 ② 가위 ③ 가왜 ④ 가의

3 ① 앱사이트 ② 웝사이트 ③ 웹사이트 ④ 윕사이트

9 Select the correct pronunciation of 삶이.

① [사리] ② [살미] ③ [삼미] ④ [사미]

10 Select the correct pronunciation of 좋아요.

① [조하요] ② [조다요] ③ [조사요] ④ [조아요]

ANSWER

1 ① 나 ② 도 ③ 레 ④ 미 ⑤ 새
2 ① 저 ② 그 ③ 요 ④ 추 ⑤ 귀
3 ① 봄 ② 한국 ③ 경찰 ④ 집안
4 ① 끝 ② 짜 ③ 빵 ④ 씨 ⑤ 때
5 ① 피부(skin) ② 주유소(gas station) ③ 소원(wish) ④ 행복(happiness) ⑤ 관심(interest)
　 pi-bu 　　　 ju-yu-so 　　　 so-won 　　　 haeng-bok 　　　 gwan-sim
6 ③ **7** ④
8 1. ① 2. ② 3. ③
9 ② **10** ④

Notes on Romanization

The romanization of Korean words, phrases, and sentences in this book mostly follows the standardized form. To reflect pronunciations closer to English, the consonant ㄹ is represented as "r" when combined with compound vowels, and the consonant ㅅ is represented as "sh" when combined with compound vowels. Consonant assimilation phenomena are also reflected in the romanization. For accurate pronunciation in Korean, please refer to the audio recording.

CHAPTER 2

존댓말 vs 반말
Polite vs. Casual Language

안녕하세요.

Now that you've mastered
how to read and write Hangeul,
it's time to dive into learning
Korean phrases and sentences.
You can also use this chapter to further
practice reading Hangeul.

Understanding Politeness Levels in Korean

Before learning basic expressions and how to form short and long sentences, the first thing you need to know is that there are two different forms of speaking Korean:

① **존댓말**, polite language (also known as "formal
jon-daen-mal
speech" or "honorific language") and

② **반말**, casual language (also known as "informal
ban-mal
speech.")

존댓말, or polite language, is used when
jon-daen-mal
addressing people you've met for the first time, who are older than you, or whomever you wish to show special courtesy. It can also be used with anyone you aren't close enough to use casual speech with.

반말, or casual language, is used when
ban-mal
speaking with someone of the same age or younger, or anyone you feel close and comfortable enough to use casual speech with.

In reality, people flexibly adjust their language based on the context of the situation. For example, in a school setting, when students are in the same grade or of the same age, it's common for them to use casual language, even when meeting for the first time. Similarly, in a professional setting, it's common to use polite language with coworkers, regardless of how close you are outside of work or their age.

It also depends on the closeness level with the person you're talking to. Just because your family members are older, it doesn't mean you have to use polite language with them. Many people feel comfortable using casual language with their family because they're close.

Ultimately, the choice of speech style often depends on what individuals find most appropriate and comfortable in different relationships, interactions, or settings.

Given the flexibility between polite speech and casual language, it's recommended to become comfortable using both forms of speech.

1. 존댓말 (Polite Language)

Polite speech is commonly categorized into two types: sentences ending with
-요 and those ending with -니다.
(yo)   (ni-da)

(The distinction between these two endings lies in the level of formality; generally,
-니다 is considered more formal than -요. But this doesn't mean you should
(ni-da)   (yo)
only reserve -니다 for formal occasions. In everyday conversations, many people
(ni-da)
interchangeably use both -니다 and -요 endings when using polite language.
(ni-da)   (yo)
Therefore, it's okay not to overly differentiate between them in practice.)

For example, in polite language, we say "Hello" as 안녕하세요.
(an-nyeong-ha-se-yo)

"Thank you" can be expressed as 고마워요/고맙습니다 or 감사해요/감사합니다.
(go-ma-wo-yo) (go-map-seum-ni-da)   (gam-sa-hae-yo) (gam-sa-ham-ni-da)

"Sorry" is 미안해요/미안합니다 or 죄송해요/죄송합니다.
(mi-an-hae-yo) (mi-an-ham-ni-da)   (joe-song-hae-yo) (joe-song-ham-ni-da)

As you can see in each expression, most of them end with -요 or -니다 which
represents they are polite language.

By observing the way a sentence ends, most of the time you can differentiate
between polite and casual language.

Of course, there are some exceptions. Take, for example, the Korean polite
expressions for "Yes," which are 네/예 (예 sounds more formal than 네.)
(ne) (ye)
Even though they don't follow the usual -니다 or -요 pattern, these expressions are
so brief and common that you shouldn't have much trouble remembering them.

Meanwhile, "No" in the polite language are 아니요/아닙니다, which do follow
(a-ni-yo) (a-nim-ni-da)
the pattern.

2. 반말 (Casual Language)

Then what about casual language, 반말?
ban-mal

In casual language, there is no specific ending like in polite language, so if a sentence doesn't end with -요 or -니다, it is usually a casual language. Since 반말 doesn't have
ban-mal
its unique ending, it's shorter than its polite counterpart in most cases.

In casual language, you can use 안녕 to say "Hello" or "Hi."
an-nyeong

"Thank you" is 고마워 and "Sorry" is 미안해.
go-ma-wo   mi-an-hae

As you can see, both of them have 요 removed from the polite forms.

However, you cannot use 감사해 for "Thank you" or 죄송해 for "Sorry" in casual language, because the words 감사 and 죄송 are reserved for polite expressions.
gam-sa   joe-song
This highlights that it's not just about sentence endings; certain words are exclusive to either polite or casual language.

"Yes" and "No" are 응 and 아니 respectively.
eung   a-ni

 In a Nutshell

	존댓말 (Polite Langauge)	반말 (Casual Language)
Hello, Hi	안녕하세요	안녕
Thank you	고마워요, 고맙습니다	고마워
	감사해요, 감사합니다	
Sorry	미안해요, 미안합니다	미안해
	죄송해요, 죄송합니다	
Yes	네, 예	응
No	아니요, 아닙니다	아니

→ 존댓말 mostly ends with either -요 or -니다. 반말 doesn't have its own unique ending and is shorter than the 존댓말 counterpart.

1   Listen to the dialogue and check ☑ whether each sentence is polite or casual. (You can simply pay attention to how the sentence ends, without having to understand the full sentence.)

⊙ TRACK 075

여자

☐ POLITE / ☐ CASUAL

남자

☐ POLITE / ☐ CASUAL

여자

☐ POLITE / ☐ CASUAL

남자

☐ POLITE / ☐ CASUAL

VOCABULARY	TRANSLATION			ANSWER	
여자 : woman _{yeo-ja}	Ⓐ	Woman	I'm sorry.	Ⓐ	Polite, Polite
		Man	It's okay.	Ⓑ	Polite, Polite
남자 : man _{nam-ja}	Ⓑ	Woman	Bye.	Ⓒ	Polite, Casual
		Man	Bye.	Ⓓ	Polite, Casual

VOCABULARY

학생 : student
hak-saeng

선생님 : teacher
seon-saeng-nim

저 : I (polite)
jeo

나 : I (casual)
na

TRANSLATION

C Student Hello, Miss!
   Teacher Hi!

D Student I'm Minjoo Kim. What about you, Miss?
   Teacher I am teacher Vicky. Nice to meet you.
   Student Nice to meet you too, Miss!

Basic Expressions in Korean

2

In this chapter, let's move beyond simply telling the difference between polite and casual speech. We'll explore a variety of expressions, their literal meanings and the specific situations in which they are used.

1. Greetings and Farewells

(A) Greetings

Do you remember how to say "Hello" or "Hi" in Korean?

In polite language, it's 안녕하세요. In casual language it's 안녕.

an-nyeong-ha-se-yo   an-nyeong
These are the most common Korean greeting.

안녕 means "peace" or "well-being," and 하세요 is derived from

an-nyeong   ha-se-yo
하다 meaning "to do."

ha-da

Originally, 안녕하세요 and 안녕 are in the form of a question with a question mark.

an-nyeong-ha-se-yo   an-nyeong
Therefore, they literally translate to "Are you at peace?" or "Are you in well-being?"

Now it has become common to use it without the question mark, and it's used simply to greet people, like "Hello." So, when someone says 안녕하세요,

an-nyeong-ha-se-yo
you can respond with a friendly 안녕하세요 in return.

an-nyeong-ha-se-yo

In Korean, greetings like "Good morning," "Good afternoon," and "Good evening" are not as commonly used as in English. If you must say it in Korean, you can say,

좋은 아침*이에요 for "Good morning,"
jo-eun   a-chi-mi-e-yo

좋은 오후*예요 for "Good afternoon," and
jo-eun   o-hu-ye-yo

좋은 저녁*이에요 for "Good evening."
jo-eun   jeo-nyeo-gi-e-yo

Each of them literally means, "It's a good morning,"

"It's a good afternoon," and "It's a good evening."

* 아침 : morning
  a-chim
* 오후 : afternoon
  o-hu
* 저녁 : evening
  jeo-nyeok

However, it's recommended to stick with the more common and widely used

안녕하세요 in most situations. Same applies to its casual form, 안녕.
an-nyeong-ha-se-yo   an-nyeong

Short Dialogue ▶ **TRACK 076**

빅키 선생님, 안녕하세요.

안녕!

학생   선생님

◀️ⓑ▶ Farewells

❶ 존댓말 (Polite Language)

When bidding farewell in polite language, there are two common ways to say goodbye:

1. 안녕히 가세요
an-nyeong-hi   ga-se-yo

2. 안녕히 계세요
an-nyeong-hi   gye-se-yo

Both mean "Bye," but they are used in slightly different scenarios, depending on whether the person you're saying goodbye to is leaving or staying.

The first, **안녕히 가세요**, literally means "peacefully(안녕히) go (가세요)."
an-nyeong-hi   ga-se-yo
It is used when the other person is leaving.

The second, **안녕히 계세요**, literally means "peacefully(안녕히) stay(계세요)."
an-nyeong-hi   gye-se-yo
It is used when the other person is staying.

For a clearer understanding, let's look at a few practical scenarios:

Short Dialogue

▶️ TRACK 077

After finishing dinner with someone, you both need to go home. In this situation, as you are both leaving, you bid farewell with
안녕히 가세요
an-nyeong-hi ga-se-yo
to each other.

안녕히 가세요.

You've been enjoying your time at someone's house, and now it's time to leave. Since the host is staying behind in their own home, you would bid them farewell with **안녕히 계세요**, and
an-nyeong-hi gye-se-yo
they would respond to you with **안녕히 가세요.**
an-nyeong-hi ga-se-yo

▶ TRACK 078

안녕히 가세요.

안녕히 계세요.

When ending an online video chat, since both participants are essentially leaving the online platform, **안녕히 가세요** is the
an-nyeong-hi ga-se-yo
most common and natural choice.

▶ TRACK 079

안녕히 가세요!

안녕히 가세요!

❷ 반말 (Casual Language)

The casual forms for "Goodbye" are **잘 가** and **잘 있어**. You can also just use **안녕**.
jal ga   jal i-sseo   an-nyeong

1. **잘 가** literally means "go well," and its polite counterpart
   jal ga
   would be **안녕히 가세요**, with both expressions having the
   an-nyeong-hi ga-se-yo
   same usage; it is used for someone who is leaving.

2. **잘 있어** literally means "stay well," and its polite counterpart
   jal i-sseo
   would be **안녕히 계세요**, with both expressions having
   an-nyeong-hi gye-se-yo
   the same usage; it is used for someone who is staying.

3. **안녕** can not only be used for greetings but also farewells.
   an-nyeong

◀ⓒ▶ Good night

When you're parting at night, you can say goodbye by wishing someone a good sleep.

The Korean version of "Good night" is "Sleep well."

In polite form, you would say **안녕히 주무세요**,
                              an-nyeong-hi ju-mu-se-yo
which literally translates to "Peacefully sleep."

In casual form, you would say **잘 자**, which literally translates to "Sleep well."
                               jal ja

 **In a Nutshell**

⊙ TRACK 080

	존댓말 (Polite Langauge)	반말 (Casual Language)
Hello, Hi	안녕하세요	안녕
Bye	안녕히 가세요 안녕히 계세요	안녕 잘 가 잘 있어
Good night	안녕히 주무세요	잘 자

2. Yes and No

In polite language, "Yes" is 네 or 예.

(예 sounds more formal than 네, so saying 네 is more common than 예.)

In casual language, it is 응.

For "No," it's 아니요 in polite, and 아니 in casual language.

There is one interesting difference between English's Yes and No and those of Korean.

For example, if someone asks, "Haven't you eaten?" in English,
and you really haven't eaten, your response would be "No, I haven't,"
as it negates the action of eating.

In Korean, however, responding with "Yes(네), I haven't" would be
appropriate since you are acknowledging the fact of
not having eaten stated in the question.

This is because in English, you can respond with "Yes"
if your response is a positive sentence,
and "No" if your response is a negative sentence,
regardless of what the other person says. But in Korean, saying "Yes"
always implies approval, acknowledgment or agreement
with the other person's remarks, and "No" is always for disapproval,
denial and disagreement.

Therefore, you can think of 네 as more like "Sure,"

ne

"What you said is true," or "I agree," and 아니요 as "No, you can't,"

a-ni-yo

"What you said is not true," or "I don't agree."

 **In a Nutshell**

	존댓말 **(Polite language)**	반말 **(Casual language)**
Yes (agreement, approval)	네, 예	응
No (disagreenment, disapproval)	아니요	아니

Practice Quiz

Let's do some practice by choosing the most natural response for Person B in each dialogue.

1   **Person B is busy. How would he respond to A's question in Korean?**

A: Are you busy?

B: 네 ☐ / 아니요 ☐
   ne   a-ni-yo

2   **Person B doesn't like pickles. How would he respond to A's question in Korean?**

A: You don't like pickles?

B: 응 ☐ / 아니 ☐
   eung   a-ni

3   **Person B is Korean. How would he respond to A's question in Korean?**

A: You are not Korean?

B: 네 ☐ / 아니요. ☐ I am Korean.
   ne   a-ni-yo

4   **Person B doesn't want Person A to call him now.**

A: Can I call you now?

B: 응 ☐ / 아니 ☐
   eung   a-ni

ANSWER

1 네 (because Person B is saying that what Person A said is true.)
   ne

2 응 (because Person B is saying that what Person A said is true.)
   eung

3 아니요 (because Person B is saying that what Person A said is not true.)
   a-ni-yo

4 아니 (because Person B is expressing disapproval of what Person A asked.)
   a-ni

네's Diverse Usages
ne

Aside from expressing agreement or consent, 네 has other usages too.
ne

❶ "I see," or "Okay, go on"

〈Conversation between a customer service staff and a customer〉

Customer: Hello, is this the customer center?

Staff: 네, 맞아요. (Yes, that's right.)
     ne ma-ja-yo

Customer: I'm calling to ask you something.

Staff: 네. (I see.)
     ne

Customer: I recently bought a pair of jeans from your store.

Staff: 네. (Okay, go on.)
     ne

Customer: But it doesn't fit me. Can I get an exchange?

Staff: 네, 그럼요. (Sure, of course.)
     ne geu-leom-yo

---

* More Expressions of Agreement

맞아요 : That's right. You're right.
ma-ja-yo

그럼요 : Of course.
geu-leom-yo

알겠어요 : Alright. / Gotcha. / I will do.
al-ge-sseo-yo

좋아요 : Okay, I'd like that.
jo-a-yo

그래요 : Okay, let's do that.
geu-lae-yo

❷ "Pardon?"

〈Conversation between a foreign tourist and a local Korean〉

Foreign Tourist: Can you speak English?

Korean: 네? (Pardon?)
     ne

❸ "You're welcome."

It's also a common response to "Thank you" in Korean. We'll explore more details in the very next pages!

3. "Thank you" and "You're welcome"

◖ A ◗ Thank you

There are 4 ways to say "Thank you" in polite language. In the order of formality, it goes like this :

감사합니다
gam-sa-ham-ni-da
Most Formal

고맙습니다
go-map-seum-ni-da

감사해요
gam-sa-hae-yo

고마워요
go-ma-wo-yo
Least Formal

* Expressions or sentences ending in - 니다
are generally more formal than those ending in -요.

Then, what is the difference between 감사합니다 / 감사해요 and
gam-sa-ham-ni-da   gam-sa-hae-yo

고맙습니다 / 고마워요? In terms of meaning, there is no difference;
go-map-seum-ni-da   go-ma-wo-yo

all these expressions are used to express gratitude to someone. They are also equally common.

The only difference lies in their origin.

감사(gratitude) is a word that originates from Chinese characters, making
감사합니다 / 감사해요 Sino-Korean expressions. On the other hand, the word
고맙다 (to be thankful) which 고맙습니다 / 고마워요 stem from is a native Korean word, making them native Korean expressions.

In Korean, words are categorized into three groups:
those derived from Chinese characters (Sino-Korean), those purely originating from Korean (pure Korean or native Korean), and loanwords from languages other than Korean. While loanwords are often recognizable due to their similarity to English, distinguishing between Sino-Korean and native Korean requires specific learning and practice. We'll explore more details on this distinction in Chapter 3.

 **In a Nutshell**

"Thank you" in Korean	Sino-Korean	Native Korean
Polite & More Formal	감사합니다	고맙습니다
Polite & Less Formal	감사해요	고마워요
Casual	*	고마워

* You cannot use 감사해 for "Thank you" in casual language, because the word 감사 is reserved for polite expressions only.

◀B▶ How to Respond to "Thank you"

Do you remember 네 (Yes) from the previous chapter? 네 is one way you can respond
to "Thank you."

Responding with "Yes" to someone's expression of gratitude might seem a bit cold
and strange, but 네 actually acknowledges and gratefully accepts the other person's
expression of thanks. In English, it can be likened to saying "Sure" or "My Pleasure."

You can also respond with "No" to thank you, to humbly suggest that what you did
wasn't a big deal. It's similar to saying "Don't mention it" or "No problem" in English.

However, the form of "No" is different from 아니요/아니, the ones we learned in
the previous pages. It is actually 아니에요 in polite language and 아니야 in casual
language. 아니요/아니 simply means "No," whereas 아니에요/아니야 is
closer to "It's not."

아니에요 comes from its base form 아니다 which means "to be not."
The details of 아니에요/아니야 will be covered in Chapter 2-3.

You can also respond with **괜찮습니다 / 괜찮아요 / 괜찮아** which means "It's okay."
gwaen-chan-seum-ni-da gwaen-cha-na-yo gwaen-cha-na

It comes from the original verb **괜찮다**, which means "to be okay."
gwae-chan-ta

 In a Nutshell

⊙ TRACK 083

Responding to "Thank you"	존댓말 (Polite Language)	반말 (Casual Language)
Yes (Sure, My pleasure)	네	응
No (Don't mention it, No problem)	아니에요	아니야
It's okay	괜찮습니다, 괜찮아요	괜찮아

How about 천만에요?
cheon-ma-ne-yo

You will see that online translation tools often translate "You're welcome"

as 천만에요 in Korean. However, it's rarely used in daily life. Therefore, it's
cheon-ma-ne-yo

generally NOT recommended to use 천만에요 as a response to "Thank you"
cheon-ma-ne-yo

in everyday conversations.

4. "I'm sorry" and "It's okay"

(A) I'm sorry

There are 4 ways to say "I'm sorry" in polite language.

죄송합니다
joe-song-ham-ni-da

죄송해요
joe-song-hae-yo

미안합니다
mi-an-ham-ni-da

미안해요
mi-an-hae-yo

죄송합니다 vs 미안합니다, what's the difference?
joe-song-ham-ni-da   mi-an-ham-ni-da

죄송합니다/죄송해요 often carries a deeper sense of formality
joe-song-ham-ni-da joe-song-hae-yo
and sincerity compared to 미안합니다/미안해요. It's often used
mi-an-ham-ni-da   mi-an-hae-yo
in situations where a higher level of politeness is desired or when
emphasizing a genuine acknowledgement of wrongdoing. However,
this doesn't mean that using 미안합니다/미안해요 sounds like
a half-hearted apology. You can still use it and genuinely feel apologetic.
The difference lies in the fact that expressions containing 미안 are often
used when apologizing to individuals for whom you may feel less need
for formal politeness, such as close colleagues, or those who are much
younger than you.

For instance, when apologizing to customers who visit your store, it's
more appropriate to use 죄송합니다/죄송해요. But when a senior
colleague, who is much older than you, apologizes to you at work, they
would typically use 미안합니다/미안해요.

"I'm sorry" in Korean	Sino-Korean	Native Korean
Polite	죄송합니다 죄송해요	미안합니다 미안해요
Casual	*	미안해

* You cannot use 죄송해 for "I'm sorry" in casual language,

because the word 죄송 is reserved for polite expressions only.

◀ Ⓑ ▶ How to Respond to "I'm sorry"

You can respond with 괜찮습니다/괜찮아요 in polite language,
gwaen-chan-seum-ni-dagwaen-cha-na-yo

and 괜찮아 in casual language. They mean "It's okay" and can be used as a response
gwaen-cha-na

to both "Thank you" and "I'm sorry."

Another way is by saying 아니에요/아니야, which literally means "It's not."
a-ni-e-yo   a-ni-ya

It's like saying "No worries" or that there is nothing to apologize. This can also

be used as a response to both "Thank you" and "I'm sorry."

Responding to "I'm sorry"	존댓말 (Polite Language)	반말 (Casual Language)
It's okay	괜찮습니다 괜찮아요	괜찮아
No worries	아니에요	아니야

5. Excuse me

⊙ TRACK 086

In Korean, the expression for "Excuse me" varies depending on the situation.

❶ When navigating through crowds

잠시 means "a moment," and 만 means
"only." So, its literal translation is
"Just a moment." While it's used to ask
for someone's patience for a brief moment,
it can also be used to ask for understanding
when passing someone by.

❷ When trying to get someone's attention

저기 means "there," so it's like
saying "Hey you, over there."
It doesn't sound rude in Korean
and is a common way to get
someone's attention that you
are not acquainted with, such as
strangers, store staffs or waiters.

③ When interrupting someone

실례 means "discourtesy." By saying 실례합니다, you're
sil-lye   sil-lye-ham-ni-da
literally expressing, "I'm doing discourtesy." It is typically used
when someone is in the middle of something and you need to
interrupt briefly. For example, you can say this when knocking on
someone's door, or when someone's in the middle of a meeting or
call.

"Excuse me" is mostly used for strangers or in formal situations,
so there isn't a casual version of this expression.

1   How do you say "Hello" in Korean?

① 안녕하세요
an-nyeong-ha-se-yo

② 안녕히 가세요
an-nyeong-hi   ga-se-yo

③ 안녕히 계세요
an-nyeong-hi   gye-se-yo

④ 안녕히 주무세요
an-nyeong-hi   ju-mu-se-yo

2   What are TWO ways to use 안녕 in casual speech?
an-nyeong

① Saying "Hello"

② Saying "Goodbye"

③ Saying "Thank you"

④ Saying "I'm sorry"

3   You and your guest are saying goodbye. You are staying at your home, and your guest is leaving your home. What should you and your guest say respectively as a goodbye?

You   : 안녕히 (   ).

Your guest : 안녕히 (   ).

4   Select one mistmatched pair of 반말(casual) and 존댓말(polite language).

① 잘 자   –   안녕히 주무세요

② 잘 가   –   안녕히 가세요

③ 잘 있어   –   안녕히 계세요

④ 감사해   –   감사합니다

5   Select the most natural response for each situation.

    ① Person B speaks Korean.

       A: Do you speak Korean?

       B: 네 / 아니요.
           ne   a-ni-yo

    ② Person B doesn't like milk.

       A: Do you like milk?

       B: 응 / 아니.
           eung   a-ni

    ③ Person B isn't going to work today.

       A: You are not going to work today?

       B: 네 / 아니요.
           ne   a-ni-yo

6   Assemble the following expressions of gratitude in the order of formality (from most formal to least.)

고마워 , 고맙습니다 , 고마워요

Most Formal   _____→ Least Formal

7   What is NOT a natural response to "Thank you?"

    ① 아니에요
       a-ni-e-yo

    ② 아니요
       a-ni-yo

    ③ 괜찮아요
       gwaen-cha-na-yo

8 What is NOT the expression where 괜찮아요 can be used as a response?
gwaen-cha-na-yo

① 죄송해요
joe-song-hae-yo

② 미안해요
mi-an-hae-yo

③ 잘 자요
jal   ja-yo

9 What is the correct way to say "I'm sorry" in 반말(casual form)?

① 미안해   ② 죄송해

10 How do you say "Excuse me" when navigating through crowds?

① 저기요   ② 잠시만요
jeo-gi-yo   jam-si-man-yo

ANSWER

1 ①

2 ①, ②

3 가세요, 계세요

4 ④ (The word 감사 is reserved for polite expressions only.
The correct one would be 고마워, instead of 감사해.)

5 ① 네   ② 아니   ③ 네 (You're acknowledging what A said is true.)

6 고맙습니다 > 고마워요 > 고마워

7 ②

8 ③

9 ①

10 ②

3   Basic Korean Sentences

In this chapter, let's learn to construct basic sentences beyond fixed phrases.

Audio files aren't provided for the sentence practice sections, but it's highly encouraged to write and pronounce the sentences yourself while following the explanations.

1. I am~, We are~

◀Ⓐ▶ The pronouns "I," and "We"

Let's first learn how to say "I" and "We" in both polite and casual languages.

In English, "I" takes different forms for the subject and object; "I" and "Me."

In Korean, there is no such distinction. The only distinction is between polite and casual language.

> "I, Me" in Polite Language : 저
> jeo
> "I, Me" in Causal Language : 나
> na

The same applies to "We." There is no distinction between its subject and object form, like "We" and "Us" in English. The only distinction is between polite and causal language.

> "We, Us" in Polite Language : 저희
> jeo-hui
> "We, Us" in Casual Language : 우리
> u-li

 **In a Nutshell**

⊙ **TRACK 087**

	존댓말 (Polite Language)	반말 (Casual Language)
I, Me	저	나
We, Us	저희	우리

◀Ⓑ▶ How to say, "I am something" and "We are something"

Now, let's practice creating simple sentences using "I" and "We."

We'll start with the most basic pattern of "I am something" or "We are something."

Let's begin with a polite form.

❶ 존댓말(Polite Language)

1) 예요/이에요

Let's take this sentence : "I am a student."

In English, the word order goes :

I	am	a student
①	②	③

In Korean, it should be :

I	student *	am
①	②	③

* Note that Korean doesn't have articles, so "a" is removed.

When you finish this book and start studying grammar more extensively, you'll learn that in Korean sentences, verbs are placed at the very end. For now, just remembering "Korean verbs come at the end" will be helpful enough.

Now, let's create the Korean sentence that means "I am a student."

I	student	am

Just like in English, a subject comes first in a Korean sentence.

So we'll insert 저(I) in the first box.

저
jeo

저
jeo

What is a subject in a sentence?

A subject is the component that indicates who or what the sentence is mainly about. It is often a noun or pronoun that carries out the action or is the main focus of the sentence, and it usually appears at the beginning of a sentence. In the sentence "I am a student," "I" functions as the subject.

In the next box, we'll insert 학생, which means "student."

hak-saeng

저 학생
jeo hak-saeng

Lastly, we need to include the verb that corresponds to "am." What "am" means is the subject and the noun are equated; it identifies the subject with a particular noun.

In Korean, this can be expressed using 예요 or 이에요 which indicates the

ye-yo   i-e-yo
equality between the subject and the following noun; 저 and 학생 in this case. It is

jeo   hak-saeng
important to remember that 예요 or 이에요 is always placed after a noun.

ye-yo   i-e-yo

Then, when do we use 예요 and 이에요 respectively?

ye-yo   i-e-yo
 ① If the last syllable of the preceding noun ends with a vowel, you put 예요.
 ② If the last syllable of the preceding noun ends with a consonant, you put 이에요.

In the sentence we are creating, the noun that comes before 예요 or 이에요 is

ye-yo   i-e-yo
학생(student). The last syllable of 학생 is 생, and we can see that it ends with

hak-saeng   hak-saeng
the consonant ㅇ.

Therefore, you can put 이에요 in the last box.
i-e-yo

The complete sentence is:

저 학생이에요.*
jeo   hak-saeng-i-e-yo

* There should be no space between the noun and 예요/이에요, making 학생이에요 the correct expression, not 학생 이에요.

Topic Markers and Subject Markers

Both 저 학생이에요 and 저는 학생이에요 are correct.

The 는 in 저는 is called a topic marker, which is used to mark the topic or subject in a sentence. It is also known as a subject marker. There are diverse usages of the topic/subject markers, and we won't cover them in detail in this book. For now, just remember that it's acceptable and common for topic/subject markers to be omitted, especially while speaking.

In this book, you'll learn sentences with subject markers omitted.

Let's create another Korean sentence "We are friends."

The sentence order would go,

We	friend *	are
①	②	③

* In Korean, general nouns are spoken in singular form. Plural form is used only when referring to specific individuals. That is why the singular form "friend" will be used instead of the plural form in this sentence.

We	friend	are

First, you can insert **저희** in the first box, which corresponds to "We" in polite
jeo-hui
language.

저희
jeo-hui

Next, you can insert **친구** which means "friend" in Korean.
chin-gu

저희 친구
jeo-hui   chin-gu

Now, it's time for the last element, which indicates that the subject and the
following noun are equated. As we learned, you can use either **예요** or **이에요**,
ye-yo   i-e-yo
for this. Then which one would be correct this time?

The preceding noun **친구** (friend) ends with a vowel **ㅜ**. Since it ends with
chin-gu
a vowel, it should be followed by **예요**.
ye-yo

So, the complete sentence is:

저희 친구예요. *
jeo-hui   chin-gu-ye-yo

* There should be no space between the noun and **예요/이에요**.

2) 입니다

Besides **예요/이에요**, there's another form you can use, and that is **입니다**.

Both are **존댓말** (polite language); **예요/이에요** is a -**요** ending form,
jon-daen-mal   ye-yo   i-e-yo
whereas **입니다** is a -**니다** ending form. -**니다** sounds more formal compared
im-ni-da
to -**요**, as we learned earlier in this book.

As for **입니다**, you can attach it to any noun, regardless of whether the noun ends
im-ni-da
with a vowel or consonant.

저 학생입니다.
jeo hak-saeng-im-ni-da
= I am a student.

저희 친구입니다.
jeo-hui chin-gu-im-ni-da
= We are friends.

❷ 반말 (Casual Language) — 야/이야

Then how about its casual form?

It also takes on two different forms, based on the last syllable of the preceding noun.

① If the last syllable of the preceding noun ends with a vowel,
you put **야** after a noun.

② If the last syllable of the preceding noun ends with a consonant,
you put **이야** after a noun.

With this in mind, let's change **저 학생이에요**(I am a student) and
jeo hak-saeng-i-e-yo
저희 친구예요(We are friends) into casual forms.
jeo-hui chin-gu-ye-yo

저 학생이에요.
jeo hak-saeng-i-e-yo
(polite)

① Change **저** to **나**, which is a casual way to say "I."
jeo na
② Keep **학생** unchanged since there's no distinction between polite and casual
hak-saeng
forms for the word.

③ Decide between **야** or **이야**. Since **학생** ends with a consonant, **이야** is the
ya i-ya hak-saeng i-ya
correct choice.

나 학생이야.
na hak-saeng-i-ya
(casual)

저희 친구예요.
jeo-hui chin-gu-ye-yo

(polite)

① Change 저희 to 우리, which is a casual way to say "We."
       jeo-hui   u-li

② Keep 친구 unchanged since there's no distinction between polite and casual forms
      chin-gu
   for the word.

③ Since 친구 ends with a vowel, put 야.
       chin-gu   ya

➡ 우리 친구야.
   u-li   chin-gu-ya

(casual)

 **In a Nutshell**

It is Noun.		존댓말 (-요 ending)	존댓말 (-니다 ending)	반말
Noun (that ends with a vowel)	**+**	예요	입니다	야
Noun (that ends with a consonant)		이에요	입니다	이야

Frequently Asked Questions

1. How about other person pronouns?

The person pronouns in Korean work quite differently from English. Except for "I" and "We," there isn't a direct equivalent for "You," "He," "She," and "They." While we do have those pronouns, there are various alternatives depending on the age or closeness level of the person you're addressing or referring to.

At the absolute beginner stage, you don't necessarily have to worry about the details on pronouns. You will get to learn them in detail in an extensive grammar book.

2. I've seen sentences without a subject. Is it okay to omit it?

Yes. In Korean, when the subject is contextually obvious, it is often omitted. For instance, when introducing or responding to questions about yourself, it's evident that you are talking about yourself. In such cases, it's perfectly fine to say 학생이에요
                                                                        hak-saeng-i-e-yo
instead of 저 학생이에요. This applies not only to 저 but to all other subjects.
        jeo hak-saeng-i-e-yo   jeo

Let's practice making more sentences with 예요/이에요, 입니다 and 야/이야.
We'll start by learning how to say basic nouns, such as "this" and "that."

◀Ⓐ▶ This, That

❶ This

> This (modifier) : 이
>   i
> This (noun) : 이거, 이것
>   i-geo   i-geot

In English, "this" can function both as a noun and as a modifier.

In the example "I like this," the word "this" functions as a noun, specifically referring
to "this one." On the other hand, in "I like this book," "this" functions as a modifier that
modifies* the noun "book."

* In grammar, to modify means to add information to a word, often to provide
  more detail or specificity.

However, in Korean, the "this" when used as a noun and the "this" when used as
a modifier are different.

이 is a modifier that means "this," and it's always paired with a particular noun
i
and cannot be used on its own.

이 남자
i   nam-ja
this man

이 여자
i   yeo-ja
this woman

이거

이 책
i chaek
this book

이 사과
i   sa-gwa
this apple

이 집
i   jip
this house

Yet, when referring to the noun "this," we literally express it as "this thing," using 이것 or 이거 in Korean. There shouldn't be a space between 이 and 거, 것
_{i-geot} _{i-geo} _i _{geo} _{geot}
because they are fixed pronouns. The same applies to the rest of the pronouns we'll explore in this chapter.

Both 거 and 것 mean "thing," and 거 is more commonly used than 것
_{geo} _{geot} _{geo} _{geot}
in spoken language. It's important to note that these words can't stand alone; they require a modifier to specify the type of "thing" they are referring to.

❷ That

There are two types of "that" in Korean.

	That	**That (over there)**
Modifier	그 _{geu}	저 _{jeo}
Noun	그거 or _{geu-geo} 그것 _{geu-geot}	저거 or _{jeo-geo} 저것 _{jeo-geot}

Let's take a look at the first "that."

> That (modifier): 그
> _{geu}
> That (noun) : 그거, 그것
> _{geu-geo} _{geu-geot}

그 is a modifier which means "that," and it's used when referring to
_{geu}
① something that's out of one's sight but in one's mind or

② something that's at a closer distance to the listener, not the speaker.

For example, if you say 그 책 (that book), it will mean either ① the book that
_{geu chaek}
I cannot see right now but the one that I remember/saw/liked/talked about, or

② the book that is located close to the other person.

그 책
geu chaek
that book

그 사과
geu sa-gwa
that apple

그 집
geu jip
that house

그 여자
geu yeo-ja
that woman

그 남자
geu nam-ja
that man

그거

Just as 이거 and 이것 mean "this" (as in, this thing), 그거 and 그것 are also nouns that
i-geo   i-geot   geu-geo   geu-geot
mean "that" (as in, that thing.) They mean either ① the thing that you have in mind or

② the thing that is located close to the other person.

Now let's take a look at the second "that," which is more like "that over there."

> That over there (modifier) : 저
>   jeo
> That over there (noun) : 저거, 저것
>   jeo-geo jeo-geot

저 is used differently from 그. It refers to something within sight but located far away
jeo   geu
from both the listener and the speaker. Therefore, it's often translated as "that over

there."

For example, if you say 저 책 (that book), it will mean the book that you can see but
                        jeo chaek
located far away.

Likewise, 저거 and 저것 will refer to "that thing" located far away.
          jeo-geo   jeo-geot

저 책
jeo chaek
that book

저 사과
jeo sa-gwa
that apple

저 집
jeo jip
that house

저 남자
jeo nam-ja
that man

저거

저 여자
jeo yeo-ja
that woman

Q: If 저 means both "I, me" and "that (over there)," how can
jeo

I determine which one is used in a particular sentence?

A: Just like many other languages, Korean also has numerous homonyms.

They can usually be understood from context, so there's no need to worry

too much about them.

 In a Nutshell

⊙ TRACK 088

	This	**That**	**That (over there)**
Modifier	이	그	저
Noun	이거 or 이것	그거 or 그것	저거 or 저것

◀ Ⓑ ▶ This is~, That is~

Now, let's use the nouns we just learned and create sentences with 예요/이에요, 입니다, and 야/이야. We'll first practice with 예요/이에요.

❶ This is a book.

❷ That is an apple.

❸ That over there is a house.

Before checking the explanations and answers below, take a moment to make the three sentences in Korean on your own.

① "This" refers to "this thing," so you can use 이거. The word "book" in
i-geo
Korean is 책. Since 책 ends with a consonant, you can put 이에요.
chaek   chaek   i-e-yo

이거 책이에요.
i-geo   chae-gi-e-yo

② "That" refers to "that thing," and it's closer to the listener, so you can
use 그거. The word "apple" in Korean is 사과. Since 사과 ends with a
geu-jeo   sa-gwa   sa-gwa
vowel, you can put 예요.
ye-yo

그거 사과예요.
geu-geo   sa-gwa-ye-yo

③ "That" refers to "that thing over there," and it's far away, so you can
use 저거. The word "house" in Korean is 집. Since 집 ends with a
jeo-geo   jip   jip
consonant, you can put 이에요.
i-e-yo

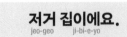

저거 집이에요.
jeo-geo   ji-bi-e-yo

Now, let's try a few more sentences. This time, you can use any of the endings you prefer among 예요/이에요, 입니다, and 야/이야. Feel free to try them on your own first before checking the explanation and answers.

❹ This man is a student.

The "this" in "this man" is a modifier. So, you can use "이."

이
i

The noun it modifies is "man." In Korean, "man" is 남자.
nam-ja

이 남자
i   nam-ja

Next comes the noun "student," which "this man" is equated to. In Korean, "student" is 학생.
hak-saeng

이 남자 학생
i   nam-ja hak-saeng

Lastly, you need to include a verb that corresponds to "is." Since 학생 ends with a consonant, you put 이에요.
hak-saeng
i-e-yo

이 남자 학생이에요.
i   nam-ja   hak-saeng-i-e-yo

Alternative Answers :

이 남자 학생입니다. (more formal)
i   nam-ja   hak-saeng-im-ni-da

이 남자 학생이야. (casual)
i   nam-ja   hak-saeng-i-ya

❺ That woman is my friend.

The "that" in "that woman" is a modifier. So, you can use 그.
geu

그
geu

The noun it modifies is "woman." In Korean, "woman" is 여자.
<small>yeo-ja</small>

그 여자
<small>geu   yeo-ja</small>

Next comes the noun "my friend," which "that woman" is equated to. In Korean, "friend" is 친구. Then how about "my?"
<small>chin-gu</small>

"My" in Korean is commonly expressed as "제." Since it's a modifier, it is followed by a noun.
<small>je</small>

(e.g. 제 책 : my book)
<small>je chaek</small>

So you can say 제 친구 for "my friend."
<small>je   chin-gu</small>

그 여자 제 친구
<small>geu   yeo-ja   je   chin-gu</small>

Lastly, you need to include a verb that corresponds to "is." Since 친구 ends with a vowel, you put 예요.
<small>chin-gu</small>
<small>ye-yo</small>

그 여자 제 친구예요.
<small>geu   yeo-ja   je   chin-gu-ye-yo</small>

Alternative Answers :

그 여자 제 친구입니다. (more formal)
<small>geu   yeo-ja   je   chin-gu-im-ni-da</small>

그 여자 내* 친구야. (casual)
<small>geu   yeo-ja   nae   chin-gu-ya</small>

* 내 means "my" in casual language.

❻ That woman over there is my girlfriend.

The "that over there" is a modifier, so you can use 저.
_{jeo}

저
jeo

The noun it modifies is "woman." As we learned, "woman" is 여자.
_{yeo-ja}

저 여자
jeo yeo-ja

Next comes the noun "my girlfriend."

To say "girlfriend" in Korean, you can combine the word "woman" and "friend,"

resulting in 여자친구. (Likewise, "boyfriend" is the combination of "man"
yeo-ja-chin-gu

and "friend," which would be 남자친구.)
nam-ja-chin-gu

Just like we learned, you can say 제 for "my" in polite language, 내 for "my"
je   nae

in casual language.

저 여자 제 여자친구
jeo yeo-ja je yeo-ja-chin-gu

저 여자 내 여자친구
jeo yeo-ja nae yeo-ja-chin-gu

Since 여자친구 ends with a vowel, you can use 예요.
yeo-ja-chin-gu   ye-yo

If you'd like to use a more formal form of polite language, you can use 입니다.
im-ni-da

If you prefer casual language, you can use 야.
ya

저 여자 제 여자친구예요.
jeo yeo-ja je yeo-ja-chin-gu-ye-yo

저 여자 제 여자친구입니다.
jeo yeo-ja je yeo-ja-chin-gu-im-ni-da

저 여자 내 여자친구야.
jeo yeo-ja nae yeo-ja-chin-gu-ya

3. is not~

Then how do we say something/somebody is "NOT" something?

❶ 존댓말 (Polite Language)

1) 아니에요

You can express that the subject is not a certain noun by placing the noun first and then adding 아니에요 afterward. 아니에요 requires a space after the preceding noun, unlike 예요/이에요. It's also important to remember that it's spelled 아니"에"요, not 아니"예"요.

저 학생 아니에요. = I am not a student.
jeo hak-saeng a-ni-e-yo
I STUDENT AM NOT

저희 친구 아니에요. = We are not friends.
jeo-hui chin-gu a-ni-e-yo
WE FRIENDS ARE NOT

이거 사과 아니에요. = This is not an apple.
i-geo sa-gwa a-ni-e-yo
THIS APPLE IS NOT

아니에요 is the present tense conjugation of 아니다 (to be not [a noun]).
a-ni-e-yo a-ni-da
All base forms of Korean verbs and adjectives end with -다, and they must be conjugated in the appropriate tense to be used in sentences. 아니에요 is an example of such conjugation, derived from 아니다. It isn't formed by combining a noun with 예요. You will learn about conjugations in detail in an extensive grammar book.

Practice Quiz

Create each Korean sentence using the words in the box.

teacher	선생님 seon-saeng-nim	man, male	남자 nam-ja
hat	모자 mo-ja	woman, female	여자 yeo-ja
book	책 chaek	fruit	과일 gwa-il
notebook	공책 gong-chaek	vegetable	채소 chae-so

1   **I am not a teacher.**

_____

2   **This is not a hat.**

_____

3   **This is not a book. It's a notebook.**

_____

4   **I am not a man. I am a woman.**

_____

5   **That is not a fruit. It's a vegetable.**

_____

ANSWER

1   저   선생님   아니에요.
    jeo   seon-saeng-nim   a-ni-e-yo

2   이거   모자   아니에요.
    i-geo   mo-ja   a-ni-e-yo

3   이거   책   아니에요.   공책이에요.*
    i-geo   chaek   a-ni-e-yo   gong-chae-gi-e-yo

4   저   남자   아니에요.   여자예요.*
    jeo   nam-ja   a-ni-e-yo   yeo-ja-ye-yo

5   그거   과일   아니에요.   채소예요.*
    geu-geo   gwa-il   a-ni-e-yo   chae-so-ye-yo

    * In the second sentence, it's okay to omit the subject because they're clearly
      referring to the same subject in the first sentence. Whether in written or spoken sentences,
      it's common to omit the subject when it's obvious from the context what the subject is.

2) 아닙니다

There's another form of "is not ~" for polite language, which is 아닙니다.
 _{a-nim-ni-da}
Since it is the -니다 ending form, it sounds more formal compared to 아니에요.
 _{a-ni-e-yo}

I'm not a student. = 저 학생 아닙니다.
 _{jeo hak-saeng a-nim-ni-da}

This is not my book. = 이거 제 책 아닙니다.
 _{i-geo je chaek a-nim-ni-da}

We are not friends. We are family. = 저희 친구 아닙니다. 가족입니다.
 _{jeo-hui chin-gu a-nim-ni-da ga-jo-gim-ni-da}

❷ 반말 (Casual Language) — 아니야

In casual language, you can use 아니야.
 _{a-ni-ya}

I'm not a student. = 나 학생 아니야.
 _{na hak-saeng a-ni-ya}

This is not my book. = 이거 내 책 아니야.
 _{i-geo nae chaek a-ni-ya}

We are not friends. We are family. = 우리 친구 아니야. 가족이야.
 _{u-li chin-gu a-ni-ya ga-jo-gi-ya}

 **In a Nutshell**

It is Noun.		존댓말 (-요 ending)	존댓말 (-니다 ending)	반말
Noun	**+**	아니에요	아닙니다	아니야

Practice Quiz

Make Korean setences in 반말(casual language).

1   **This woman is not my friend.**

_____

2   **That over there is not coffee. It's tea.**
      (coffee : 커피, tea : 차)
              keo-pi   cha

_____

3   **This man is not a student. He's a teacher.**

_____

ANSWER

1   이   여자   내   친구   아니야.
     i   yeo-ja   nae   chin-gu   a-ni-ya

2   저거   커피   아니야.   차야.*
     jeo-geo   keo-pi   a-ni-ya   cha-ya

3   이   남자   학생   아니야.   선생님이야.*
     i   nam-ja   hak-saeng   a-ni-ya   seon-saeng-ni-mi-ya

> * In the second sentence, it's okay to omit the subject because they're clearly referring
> to the same subject in the first sentence. Whether in written or spoken sentences,
> it's common to omit the subject when it's obvious from the context what the subject is.

1 Write the Korean words for "I, Me" in polite and casual language.

① I, Me (polite) :

② I, Me (casual) :

2 Select TWO words that mean "We, Us" in Korean.

① 저희 ② 제 ③ 우리 ④ 내

3 Select whether to use 예요 or 이에요 after each noun below.

① 학생( ). ② 선생님( ).
hak-saeng seon-saeng-nim
student teacher

③ 여자( ). ④ 남자( ).
yeo-ja nam-ja
woman man

⑤ 이거( ). ⑥ 책( ).
i-geo chaek
this one book

⑦ 차( ). ⑧ 집( ).
cha jip
tea, car house

4 Write the 반말(casual language) version of each sentence.

① 저 한국 사람이에요. (I'm Korean.)
jeo han-guk sa-la-mi-e-yo

(한국 사람 : a Korean person)
han-guk sa-lam

→

_____

② 저희 친구예요. (We are friends.)
jeo-hui   chin-gu-ye-yo

➡

_____

③ 이거 제 책이에요. (This is my book.)
i-geo   je   chae-gi-e-yo

➡

_____

5 Select the correctly written sentence for "This is not tea."

① 이거 차예요.   ② 이거 차아니에요.

③ 이거 차 아니에요.   ④ 이거 차 아니예요.

6 Select one sentence that does NOT mean "We are students."

① 우리 학생이야.   ② 저희 학생이에요.

③ 저희 학생입니다.   ④ 제 학생이에요.

7 Write the Korean sentence that means "This person is not my friend."
(person: 사람)

➡

_____

ANSWER

1 ① 저   ② 나
      jeo   na

2 ①, ③

3 ① 이에요   ② 이에요
   ③ 예요   ④ 예요
   ⑤ 예요   ⑥ 이에요
   ⑦ 예요   ⑧ 이에요

4 ① 나 한국 사람이야.   ② 우리 친구야.
   ③ 이거 내 책이야.

5 ③

6 ④ (④ means "(someone) is my student.")

7 이   사람   제   친구   아니에요. (polite)
   i   sa-lam   je   chin-gu   a-ni-e-yo

   이   사람   제   친구   아닙니다.
   i   sa-lam   je   chin-gu   a-nim-ni-da
   (polite and formal)

   이   사람   내   친구   아니야. (casual)
   i   sa-lam   nae   chin-gu   a-ni-ya

157

1   What is a polite language called in Korean?

① 반말
ban-mal

② 존댓말
jon-daen-mal

2   Listen to the audio and select what the speakers are doing.

▶ TRACK 089

① Saying hi

② Saying bye

③ Thanking

④ Apologizing

3   Two people are about to say goodbye. If both are leaving, what would they say to each other?

① 안녕히 계세요.
an-nyeong-hi   gye-se-yo

② 안녕히 가세요.
an-nyeong-hi   ga-se-yo

4   Listen to the audio and select the most appropriate response.

▶ TRACK 090

① 저기요.
jeo-gi-yo

② 천만에요.
cheon-ma-ne-yo

③ 괜찮아요.
gwaen-cha-na-yo

5   How do you say "Thank you" in 존댓말?
jon-daen-mal

➡

6 What is NOT 네's usage?
_{ne}

① 네. = Yes.

② 네. = I see.

③ 네? = Pardon?

④ 네. = Okay.

⑤ 네. = Excuse me.

7 How do you say "No" in 존댓말?
_{jon-daen-mal}

---

8 What is the best way to say "Excuse me" to call a waiter in a restaurant?

① 저기요
_{jeo-gi-yo}

② 잠시만요
_{jam-si-man-yo}

③ 네
_{ne}

④ 죄송합니다
_{joe-song-ham-ni-da}

9 Which word do you use to refer to something that's far away
(as in, that one over there?)

① 이거
_{i-geo}

② 그거
_{geu-geo}

③ 저거
_{jeo-geo}

[10~12] Fill in the blank with the correct modifier.

10   This person = (　　　　　) 사람
_{sa-lam}

11   That house (that we don't see right now) = (　　　　　) 집
_{jip}

12   That woman (over there) = (　　　　　) 여자
_{yeo-ja}

[13~14] Fill in the blank with either 이에요 or 예요.
_{i-e-yo}　　_{ye-yo}

13   물 (　　　　　). = It's water.
_{mul}
water

14   학교 (　　　　　). = It's a school.
_{hak-gyo}
school

[15~17] Write the following sentences in 존댓말.
_{jon-daen-mal}

15   My friend is a student.

_____

16   We are not a family.

_____

17   This is my car.

_____

[18~20] Write the following sentences in 반말.
<small>ban-mal</small>

18 I am not Korean. (Korean [person] : 한국 사람)
<small>han-guk-sa-lam</small>

➡️ _____

19 That (near the listener) is tea.

➡️ _____

20 That (over there) is a book.

➡️ _____

ANSWER

1 ②

2 ① [Audio] 남자: 선생님, 안녕하세요!
　　　　　　　 여자: 안녕!

3 ②

4 ③ [Audio] 여자: 죄송해요.

5 감사합니다, 감사해요, 고맙습니다
　　or 고마워요

6 ⑤

7 아니요 or 아닙니다

8 ①

9 ③

10 이

11 그

12 저

13 이에요

14 예요

15 제　친구　학생이에요. or 제　친구　학생입니다.
　　<small>je　chin-gu　hak-saeng-i-e-yo　　je　chin-gu　hak-saeng-im-ni-da</small>

16 저희　가족　아니에요. or 저희　가족　아닙니다.
　　<small>jeo-hui　ga-jok　a-ni-e-yo　　jeo-hui　ga-jok　a-nim-ni-da</small>

17 이거　제　차예요. or 이거　제　차입니다.
　　<small>i-geo　je　cha-ye-yo　　i-geo　je　cha-im-ni-da</small>

18 나　한국　사람　아니야.
　　<small>na　han-guk　sa-lam　a-ni-ya</small>

19 그거　차야.
　　<small>geu-geo　cha-ya</small>

20 저거　책이야.
　　<small>jeo-geo　chae-gi-ya</small>

CHAPTER 3

숫자
Numbers

Numbers are indispensable part of our lives, and you'll find yourself needing them in many situations. Although they are universal, how we read them varies across languages. This final chapter is all about Korean numbers. You can also use it to further practice reading Hangeul.

1 | What is Sino-Korean and Native Korean?

In Korean, there are two types of numbers: Sino-Korean and Native Korean. Each has distinct uses for counting and measuring different things. Learning both sets of numbers is important, as they are commonly used in everyday situations.

Before learning numbers, you'd first need to understand what Sino-Korean and Native Korean words are.

Korean can be broadly categorized into three types based on origin: Sino-Korean, Native Korean, and loanwords. Loanwords mainly consist of words borrowed from the Western languages or Japanese. In this chapter, let's focus on the difference between Sino-Korean and Native Korean.

"Sino-Korean words" refers to vocabularies based on Chinese characters, while "Native (or Pure) Korean words" are purely Korean terms without Chinese character influence.

In Chapter 2, we learned expressions for "Thank you," such as 감사합니다/감사해요
gam-sa-ham-ni-da   gam-sa-hae-yo
and 고맙습니다/고마워요. We also learned that
go-map-seum-ni-da   go-ma-wo-yo
the word 감사 in the former expression is
gam-sa
a Sino-Korean word based on Chinese characters, while 고맙다 in the latter is
go-map-da
a native Korean word.

Korean has numerous words derived from Chinese characters, which extend beyond just basic expressions and numbers. While many Sino-Korean words are more common in writing than casual conversation and can sometimes sound overly formal, it's important to note that about 30% of spoken Korean includes Sino-Korean words. This indicates their practicality in the Korean language and makes learning them worthwhile.

So, how do Chinese characters work in the Korean language?

When Chinese characters are adopted into Korean, their pronunciation changes to fit the Korean language. Since Chinese and Korean have different pronunciation systems, adapting the pronunciation is necessary for seamless use in Korean.

For example, let's look at the Chinese characters below, each of which mean "friend" and "learn/study."

	友	學
Meaning	friend	learn/study
Mandarin Pronunciation	[yǒu]	[xué]
Korean Pronunciation	우 u	학 hak

Each character has a syllable sound. In Mandarin Chinese, these characters are pronounced as "you" and "xue," whereas in Korean, they are pronounced as 우 and 학
_u _{hak}
respectively.

However, it's crucial to note that just saying 우 or 학 does not convey the complete
_u _{hak}
meanings of "friend" or "study." The unique aspect of Sino-Korean words is that individual characters represent syllables, but these syllables do not form complete words on their own. Instead, they combine with other Sino-Korean syllables to create meaningful words.

For instance, the Korean word 우정 means
_{u-jeong}
"friendship," where the first syllable 우 comes
_u
from the Chinese character for "friend." Similarly, 학 itself doesn't represent the entire
_{hak}
meaning of "study." It combines with other Sino-Korean syllables to form words like 학교,
_{hak-gyo}
meaning "school," or 학생, meaning "student."
_{hak-saeng}

In short, Chinese characters are not used in their original form in the Korean language, and only their pronunciation is adapted to Korean, often combinded with other Sino-Korean syllables to create meaningful words.

Therefore, knowing the exact Chinese characters isn't entirely necessary to grasp Korean words. It would be enough to recognize that 우 signifies "friend" and 학 "study," which will make it easier to comprehend words like 우정 (friendship), 학생 (student), and 학교 (school). Going further, you can intuitively grasp that the word 학우 refers to a "study mate," "class mate," or "fellow student."
(학: study + 우 : friend)

Of course, not every Sino-Korean syllable 우 indicates "friend." It can also represent different meanings, depending on which Chinese character it's derived from, such as "rain (from 雨)" or "the right (from 右)." In fact, there are many homonyms* in the Chinese characters, which naturally results in many homonyms in Sino-Korean words as well.

* Homonyms are words that sound the same (or spelled the same) but have different meanings.

The coexistence of Sino-Korean and Native Korean also leads to many synonyms* in Korean. For instance, both 책을 읽다 (native Korean word) and 독서하다 (Sino-Korean word) mean "to read books."

Likewise, both 혼자 공부하다 (native Korean
hon-ja gong-bu-ha-da
word) and 독학하다 (Sino Korean word) mean
do-ka-ka-da
"to self-study."

* Synonyms are words with similar meanings.

Becoming familiar with Sino-Korean syllables
can be beneficial when learning various words
including homonyms and synonyms.
You don't have to memorize the exact
Chinese characters they originate from.
Simply remembering their pronunciation
in Korean and their most common meanings
will be enough, especially at the beginning
stage. Starting with the most common
syllables and gradually gaining confidence
is a good strategy.

Now that you understand the distinctions
between Sino-Korean and Native Korean,
let's explore both sets of Korean numbers.

2 | Sino-Korean Numbers

LECTURE

Let's first start with Sino-Korean Numbers. You can consider this the first step in familiarizing yourselves with Sino-Korean vocabulary.

Sino-Korean and Native Korean numbers are generally not interchangeable; each has its own distinct usage.

Sino-Korean numbers are used in various situations, and it's not very important to remember every single usage at this stage. You can focus more on learning the numbers themselves.

Still, to help you practice applying the numbers you've learned in real life, you will also learn how to say the following using Sino-Korean numbers :

1. Talking about dates
   (days, months and so on)
2. Indicating price
3. Sharing phone numbers

This chapter covers from single-digit to five-digit numbers. Even if you're not a math enthusiast, there's no need to worry because Korean numbers aren't overly complicated. Once you've memorized the first ten numbers, the rest will become easy.

1. 1~10

Practice writing each Sino-Korean number from 1 to 10 in the table below.

▶ TRACK 091

1	일 il	일	일		
2	이 i	이	이		
3	삼 sam	삼	삼		
4	사 sa	사	사		
5	오 o	오	오		
6	육 yuk	육	육		
7	칠 chil	칠	칠		
8	팔 pal	팔	팔		
9	구 gu	구	구		
10	십 sip	십	십		

2. Two-digit Numbers

If you remember the first ten numbers, the rest becomes quite easy.

In Korean, numbers are formed by listing what each digit stands for in the number.

For example, 11 is seen as the combination of 10(십) and 1(일). So, 11 is called 십일.

Likewise, 12 is seen as the combination of 10(십) and 2(이). So, 12 is 십이.

Now, can you guess how to say 13? Simply combine 십(10) and 삼(3), and it becomes 십삼(13).

The rest follows the same pattern.

TRACK 092

11	십일 si-bil	십일	십일	
12	십이 si-bi	십이	십이	
13	십삼 sip-sam	십삼	십삼	
14	십사 sip-sa	십사	십사	
15	십오 si-bo	십오	십오	
16	십육 sim-nyuk	십육	십육	
17	십칠 sip-chil	십칠	십칠	
18	십팔 sip-pal	십팔	십팔	
19	십구 sip-gu	십구	십구	

Then, what about 20?

Just combine 2(**이**) and 10(**십**). So, 20 is **이십**.
                i   sip   i-sip

How about 21? Think of it as the combination of what each digit stands for.
So, combine 20(**이십**) and 1(**일**), and you get **이십 일**.
                i-sip   il   i-si-bil

Likewise, 22 is the combination of 20(**이십**) and 2(**이**), so it's **이십 이**.
                       i-sip   i   i-si-bi

The same pattern applies for the rest.

20	**이십** i-sip	이십	이십	
21	**이십 일** i-si-bil	이십 일	이십 일	
22	**이십 이** i-si-bi	이십 이	이십 이	
23	**이십 삼** i-sip-sam	이십 삼	이십 삼	
24	**이십 사** i-sip-sa	이십 사	이십 사	
25	**이십 오** i-si-bo	이십 오	이십 오	
26	**이십 육** i-sim-nyuk	이십 육	이십 육	
27	**이십 칠** i-sip-chil	이십 칠	이십 칠	
28	**이십 팔** i-sip-pal	이십 팔	이십 팔	
29	**이십 구** i-sip-gu	이십 구	이십 구	

172   **CHAPTER 3**   **2**   **SINO-KOREAN NUMBERS**

Now I'm sure you can guess how to say 30. It works the same as 20.

Simply combine 3(삼) and 10(십), and you get 삼십(30).
     sam   sip   sam-sip

31 is the combination of 삼십(30) and 일(1). So, it's 삼십 일.
                      sam-sip   il   sam-si-bil

▶ TRACK 094

30	삼십 sam-sip	삼십	삼십	
31	삼십 일 sam-si-bil	삼십 일	삼십 일	
32	삼십 이 sam-si-bi	삼십 이	삼십 이	
33	삼십 삼 sam-sip-sam	삼십 삼	삼십 삼	
34	삼십 사 sam-sip-sa	삼십 사	삼십 사	
35	삼십 오 sam-si-bo	삼십 오	삼십 오	
36	삼십 육 sam-sim-nyuk	삼십 육	삼십 육	
37	삼십 칠 sam-sip-chil	삼십 칠	삼십 칠	
38	삼십 팔 sam-sip-pal	삼십 팔	삼십 팔	
39	삼십 구 sam-sip-gu	삼십 구	삼십 구	

The same pattern applies to the remaining two-digit numbers as well.

40	사십 sa-sip	사십	사십	
41	사십일 sa-si-bil	사십일	사십일	
50	오십 o-sip	오십	오십	
52	오십이 o-si-bi	오십이	오십이	
60	육십 yuk-sip	육십	육십	
63	육십삼 yuk-sip-sam	육십삼	육십삼	
70	칠십 chil-sip	칠십	칠십	
74	칠십사 chil-sip-sa	칠십사	칠십사	
80	팔십 pal-sip	팔십	팔십	
85	팔십오 pal-si-bo	팔십오	팔십오	
90	구십 gu-sip	구십	구십	
96	구십육 gu-sim-nyuk	구십육	구십육	

97	**구십 칠** gu-sip- chil	구십 칠	구십 칠	
98	**구십 팔** gu-sip- pal	구십 팔	구십 팔	
99	**구십 구** gu-sip- gu	구십 구	구십 구	

Q: Why is 십육 romanized as "sim-nyuk?"

A: The reason why 십육 is pronounced as 심뉵 instead of 시뷱 is due to
<small>sim-nyuk   si-byuk</small>
native speaker preferences. Although it's not specifically mentioned
in the standard pronunciation rules of consonant assimilation, when
Koreans pronounce 십 and 육 together, they find it more comfortable to
<small>   sip   yuk</small>
pronounce it as 심뉵 than 시뷱. Rather than trying to logically understand
<small>sim-nyuk   si-byuk</small>
this phenomenon, it's best to simply accept that it happens for the
convenience of native speakers.

Practice Quiz

Write how to read each number in Korean.

1 **14**

2 **20**

3 **35**

4 **67**

5 **89**

6 **91**

ANSWER

1 십 사
sip- sa

2 이십
i-sip

3 삼십 오
sam-si- bo

4 육십 칠
yuk-sip-chil

5 팔십 구
pal-sip-gu

6 구십 일
gu-si-bil

Great job! You have now mastered one- and two-digit numbers! We will now learn how to read three-digit numbers and beyond.

If you are not yet comfortable with one- or two- digit numbers and feel like numbers beyond that could be too challenging, it's okay to skip this part for now.
In the meantime, feel free to move on to "Zero in Korean" on page 181.

3. Three-digit Numbers

First, we need to know how to say 100.

(For milestone numbers where the digit changes like 10(십), 100, 1000 and 10,000, there are specific terms.)
sip

100 is called 백.
baek

101 is the combination of 100(백) and 1(일), so it's 백 일.
baek   *il*   *bae-gil*

110 is the combination of 100(백) and 10(십), so it's 백 십.
baek   *sip*   *baek-sip*

111 is the combination of 100(백), 10(십), and 1(일), making it 백 십 일.
baek   *sip*   *il*   *baek-si-bil*

As numbers get larger, they might appear daunting, but you can simply break them down into each digit unit and list the numbers that each digit stands for.

Then what about 130? It's the combination of 100(백) and 30(삼십), so it's 백 삼십.
baek   *sam-sip*   *baek-sam-sip*

What about 149? It's the combination of 100(백), 40(사십) and 9(구),
baek   *sa-sip*   *gu*

so it's 백 사십 구.
baek-sa-sip-gu

How about numbers where the leading digit changes like 200, 300, 400?

It works the same way as two-digit numbers like 20(이십), 30(삼십), 40(사십)
and so on.
i-sip   *sam-sip*   *sa-sip*

For 200, combine 2 (이) with 100 (백).
i   *baek*

For 300, combine 3 (삼) with 100 (백).
sam   *baek*

For 400, combine 4 (사) with 100 (백).
sa   *baek*

100	백 baek	백	백	
200	이백 i-baek	이백	이백	
300	삼백 sam-baek	삼백	삼백	
400	사백 sa-baek	사백	사백	
500	오백 o-baek	오백	오백	
600	육백 yuk-baek	육백	육백	
700	칠백 chil-baek	칠백	칠백	
800	팔백 pal-baek	팔백	팔백	
900	구백 gu-baek	구백	구백	

Practice Quiz

Write how to read each number in Korean.

1 500 　　2 670 　　3 841 　　4 999

ANSWER

1 오백
　o-baek
2 670 is the combination of 600(육백) + 70(칠십), 육백 칠십
　　　　　　　　　　　　　　　　　　　　　yuk-baek chil-sip
3 841 is the combination of 800(팔백) + 40(사십) + 1(일), 팔백 사십 일
　　　　　　　　　　　　　　　　　　　　　　　　　pal-baek sa-si-bil
4 999 is the combination of 900(구백) + 90(구십) + 9(구), 구백 구십 구
　　　　　　　　　　　　　　　　　　　　　　　　　gu-baek gu-sip-gu

4. Four-digit Numbers

1,000 is **천** in Korean.
cheon

2,000 is **이천**, combining **이**(2) and **천** (1,000).
i-cheon · i · cheon

3,000 and 4,000 follow the same pattern :

3,000 = **삼 천** (3 and 1000)
sam-cheon

4,000 = **사 천** (4 and 1000)
sa-cheon

▶ **TRACK 097**

1,000	천 cheon	천	천	
2,000	이천 i-cheon	이천	이천	
3,000	삼천 sam-cheon	삼천	삼천	
4,000	사천 sa-cheon	사천	사천	
5,000	오천 o-cheon	오천	오천	
6,000	육천 yuk-cheon	육천	육천	
7,000	칠천 chil-cheon	칠천	칠천	
8,000	팔천 pal-cheon	팔천	팔천	
9,000	구천 gu-cheon	구천	구천	

The rest of the numbers work the same way as two- and three-digit numbers. You can simply list the numbers that each digit stands for.

For example, 2,024 would be **이천 이십 사**.

이천(2,000) + 이십(20) + 사(4)

7,500 would be **칠천 오백**.

칠천(7,000) + 오백(500)

5. Five-digit Numbers and Beyond

The milestone numbers like 10(**십**), 100(**백**), and 1,000(**천**), have unique names,
sip   baek   cheon

and the same goes for 10,000.

It's not **십 천** like "ten thousand" in English.
We have a separate term for 10,000 in Korean, which is **만**.
man

When you visit Korea, you'll notice that Korean currency often involves multiple zeros. 1,000 won (**천 원**[*]) is roughly 1 US dollar and 10,000 won(**만 원**[*])
cheo-nwon   ma-nwon

is around 10 US dollars. While shopping or discussing prices in Korea, you'll often come across 5-digit numbers involving "10,000(**만**)."
man

Even if the number seems too big, don't feel intimidated.
Simply list the numbers that each digit represents,
just as we've practiced with two-, three-, and four-digit numbers.

* 원 (won) is the Korean currency.

For example, 50,000 will be the combination of **오**(5) and **만**(10,000),
o   man

which is **오만**.
o-man

56,000 will be the combination of **오만**(50,000) and **육천**(6,000),
o-man   yuk-cheon

which is **오만 육천**.
o-man   yuk-cheon

If you're curious about numbers beyond that, feel free to check out the box below.

1. A Hundred Thousand(100,000) in Korean = 십 만
   sim-man

   → It's a combination of 10(십) and 10,000(만).
      sip   man

2. One Million(1,000,000) in Korean = 백 만
   baeng-man

   → It's a combination of 100(백) and 10,000(만)
      baek   man

3. Ten Million(10,000,000) in Korean = 천 만
   cheon-man

   → It's a combination of 1,000(천) and 10,000(만)
      cheon   man

4. A Hundred Million(100,000,000) in Korean = 1억
   i-leok

Starting from 억, it's common to include 1(일) and
             eok   il

say 1억 instead of just 억 alone, which is different from 10(십), 100(백),
    i-leok   eok   sip   baek

1,000(천), and 10,000(만), where you can typically say them without
      cheon   man

adding 일(1). Numbers above that would be 10억(1 billion),
       il   si-beok

100억(10 billion), 1,000억(100 billion) and 1조(1 trillion).
bae-geok   cheo-neok   il-jo

Practice Quiz

Write how to read each number in Korean.

1 **1,100**

2 **2,024**

3 **3,450**

4 **5,678**

5 **9,999**

6 **40,000**

ANSWER

1 1,100 = 1,000 (천) + 100 (백) = 천 백
          cheon-baek

2 2,024 = 2,000 (이천) + 20 (이십) + 4 (사) = 이천 이십 사
          i-cheon i-sip sa

3 3,450 = 3,000 (삼천) + 400 (사백) + 50 (오십) = 삼천 사백 오십
          sam-cheon sa-baek o-sip

4 5,678 = 5,000 (오천) + 600 (육백) + 70 (칠십) + 8 (팔) = 오천 육백 칠십 팔
          o-cheon yuk-baek chil-sip pal

5 9,999 = 9,000 (구천) + 900 (구백) + 90 (구십) + 9 (구) = 구천 구백 구십 구
          gu-cheon gu-baek gu-sip gu

6 40,000 = 4 (사) and 10,000 (만) = 사만
           sa-man

6. Zero in Korean

You can say either 공 or 영. (In slang, people also refer to 0 as 빵.)
gong   yeong   bbang

In Korea, it's common for phone numbers to begin with "010." So, when reading a Korean phone number, you're almost always going to say "zero."

Let's say your phone number is 010 0912 8457. You can say,

$$0 - 1 - 0 \, (공 - 일 - 공)$$
gong   il   gong

$$0 - 9 - 1 - 2 \, (공 - 구 - 일 - 이)$$
gong   gu   il   i

$$8 - 4 - 5 - 7 \, (팔 - 사 - 오 - 칠).$$
pal   sa   o   chil

7. Months and Days in Korean

⊙ TRACK 098

❶ Months

In English, each month has a unique name, like January, February and so on. In Korean, each month is expressed by combining the number and 월(month), which is the Sino-Korean word for "month."
                                                                              wol

January is the first month, so it's called 1월 by combining
i-rwol

the number 1(일) and 월.
il   wol

Likewise, since February is the second month,

it's called 2월 by combining the number 2(이) and 월.
i-wol   i   wol

If you know all the Sino-Korean numbers from 1 to 12, you're already familiar with how to say the name of each month in Korean!

Name of Each Month :
Sino-Korean Number + 월

January 1월	February 2월	March 3월	April 4월
일월 i-rwol	이월 i-wol	삼월 sa-mwol	사월 sa-wol
May 5월	June 6월	July 7월	August 8월
오월 o-wol	유월* yu-wol	칠월 chi-rwol	팔월 pa-rwol
September 9월	October 10월	November 11월	December 12월
구월 gu-wol	시월* si-wol	십일월 si-bi-rwol	십이월 si-bi-wol

* In 6월(유월) and 10월(시월),
  yu-wol   si-wol

the numbers 6 and 10 are pronounced as 유 and 시,
                                        yu   si

not 육 and 십. These changes are made for easier pronunciation
    yuk   sip

when 육 and 십 are combined with 월.
     yuk   sip   wol

❷ Days

When expressing days in Korean, it follows a similar pattern.

You simply combine the number indicating the day with the Sino-Korean word
일, which means "day."
il

> **Name of Each Day of the Month :**
>
> **Sino-Korean Number + 일**

For example,

1st: Combine 1 and 일 = 1일.
il   i-lil

4th: Combine 4 and 일 = 4일.
il   sa-il

Likewise, for 20th, it's 20일.
i-si-bil

And for 31st, it's 31일.
sam-si-bi-lil

If you know all the Sino-Korean numbers from 1 to 31,
you're already familiar with how to say each day of the month in Korean!

12월 31일에 보자!

e.g. January 5th : 1월 5일 (일월 오일)
i-rwol o-il

February 14th : 2월 14일 (이월 십사일)
i-wol sip-sa-il

March 1st : 3월 1일 (삼월 일일)
sa-mwol i-lil

June 25th : 6월 25일 (유월 이십 오일)
yu-wol i-si-bo-il

October 9th : 10월 9일 (시월 구일)
si-wol gu-il

December 25th : 12월 25일 (십이월 이십 오일)
si-bi-wol i-si-bo-il

Days of the Week in Korean

Sunday : 일요일
i-ryo-il

Monday : 월요일
wo-ryo-il

Tuesday : 화요일
hwa-yo-il

Wednesday : 수요일
su-yo-il

Thursday : 목요일
mo-gyo-il

Friday : 금요일
geu-myo-il

Saturday : 토요일
to-yo-il

Practice Quiz

1   "July 17th" in Korean

_____

2   "November 30th" in Korean

_____

3   "It's July 17th" in 존댓말
                 jon-daen-mal

_____

4   "My birthday is November 30th." in 존댓말
                                        jon-daen-mal

(birthday : 생일)
        saeng-il

_____

ANSWER

1 7월 17일 / 칠월 십칠 일
           chi-rwol sip-chi- lil
2 11월 30일 / 십일월 삼십 일
            si-bi-rwol sam-si-bil
3 7월 17일이에요. or 7월 17일입니다. *
  chi-rwol sip-chi-li-li-e-yo chi-rwol sip-chi-li-lim-ni-da
4 제 생일 11월 30일이에요. or 제 생일 11월 30일입니다.
  je saeng-il si-bi-rwol sam-si-bi-li-e-yo   je saeng-il si-bi-rwol sam-si-bi-lim-ni-da

    * When expressing today's date, the subject is not necessary.

Native Korean Numbers

With Sino-Korean numbers completed, the only thing left in this book is mastering Native Korean Numbers. You've come a long way, and you're almost there!

In native Korean, there are only numbers from 1 to 99. For numbers 100 and above, Sino-Korean numbers are used.

Native Korean numbers are also used in various situations, with the most common one being expressing age. After learning all the numbers, you'll also learn how to express age using native Korean numbers. Let's go!

1. 1~10

Practice writing each Native Korean number from 1 to 9 in the table below.

▶ TRACK 099

1	하나 ha-na	하나	하나	
2	둘 dul	둘	둘	
3	셋 set	셋	셋	
4	넷 net	넷	넷	
5	다섯 da-seot	다섯	다섯	
6	여섯 yeo-seot	여섯	여섯	
7	일곱 il-gop	일곱	일곱	
8	여덟 yeo-deol	여덟	여덟	
9	아홉 a-hop	아홉	아홉	
10	열 yeol	열	열	

2. Two-digit Numbers

❶ from 11 to 19

For 11~19, you can simply combine 10(**열**) with the single digit number.
_{yeol}

As for 11, **열**(10) and **하나**(1) are combined, so it's **열 하나**.
_{yeol} _{ha-na} _{yeol-ha-na}

As for 12, **열**(10) and **둘**(2) are combined, so it's **열 둘**.
_{yeol} _{dul} _{yeol-dul}

It goes on like this for the rest of the numbers.

▶ TRACK 100

11	**열 하나** yeol-ha-na	열 하나	열 하나	
12	**열 둘** yeol- dul	열 둘	열 둘	
13	**열 셋** yeol- set	열 셋	열 셋	
14	**열 넷** yeol- net	열 넷	열 넷	
15	**열 다섯** yeol-da-seot	열 다섯	열 다섯	
16	**열 여섯** yeol- yeo-seot	열 여섯	열 여섯	
17	**열 일곱** yeo-lil-gop	열 일곱	열 일곱	
18	**열 여덟** yeol-yeo-deol	열 여덟	열 여덟	
19	**열 아홉** yeo-la-hop	열 아홉	열 아홉	

Just like Sino-Korean numbers, Native Korean numbers are also formed by listing what each digit of the number stands for.

❷ from 20 to 99

We'll start from numbers that are multiples of tens, like 20, 30, 40 and so on. Unlike the combinable nature of Sino-Korean counterparts, there's a unique name assigned to each number.

▶ TRACK 101

20	스물 seu-mul	스물	스물	
30	서른 seo-leun	서른	서른	
40	마흔 ma-heun	마흔	마흔	
50	쉰 shwin	쉰	쉰	
60	예순 ye-sun	예순	예순	
70	일흔 il-heun	일흔	일흔	
80	여든 yeo-deun	여든	여든	
90	아흔 a-heun	아흔	아흔	

For the remaining numbers, you simply list the numbers that each digit stands for.

For example :

22 is a combination of 20(스물) and 2(둘), so it's 스물 둘.
seu-mul   dul   seu-mul-dul

31 is a combination of 30(서른) + 1(하나), so it's 서른 하나.
seo-leun   ha-na   seo-leun ha-na

49 is a combination of 40(마흔) + 9(아홉), so it's 마흔 아홉.
ma-heun   a-hop   ma-heun a-hop

It's a common frustration shared by many learners to memorize native Korean numbers. It's challenging enough to memorize from 1 to 9, and the thought of adding another set from 10 to 90 could be a bit daunting. The silver lining is, the most commonly used numbers fall within the range of single-digit numbers to 49. For numbers 50 and beyond, you'll notice that Sino-Korean numbers are more commonly used than Native Korean numbers.

So, my suggestion is to start by getting familiar with the essential numbers from 1 to 40. You can gradually tackle the rest as you become more comfortable with numbers, so it's okay to take it easy!

Practice Quiz

Write how to read each number in Native Korean.

1 8   2 11

3 26   4 34

ANSWER

1. 여덟
   yeo-deol
2. 열 하나
   yeol ha-na
3. 스물 여섯
   seu-mul yeo-seot
4. 서른 넷
   seo-leun net

3. Age in Korean

The most common usage of Native Korean numbers is when expressing age.

The measure word(or counter) for age is 살, which you can combine with the native
number to express your age.

> ### Native Korean Number + 살
> sal

However, there's one thing you need to be aware of here. Some numbers have to
change its form when combined with measure words.

These numbers are specifically:

하나(1), 둘(2), 셋(3), 넷(4), and 스물(20).
ha-na   dul   set   net   seu-mul

When 하나 combines with a counter word, it becomes 한.
ha-na   han

For example, if you want to say "1 year old,"

it should be 한 살, not 하나 살.
han-sal

둘 changes to 두.
dul   du

셋 changes to 세.
set   se

넷 changes to 네.
net   ne

스물 changes to 스무.
seu-mul   seu-mu

For 하나(1), 둘(2), 셋(3), and 넷(4), this rule applies not only to single-digit numbers
ha-na   dul   set   net

but also to 2-digit numbers ending with 1, 2, 3, and 4.

For example:

2 years old = **두 살** (not 둘 살)
_{du- sal}

13 years old = **열 세 살** (not 열 셋 살)
_{yeol-se-sal}

24 years old = **스물 네 살** (not 스물 넷 살)
_{seu-mul-ne-sal}

31 years old = **서른 한 살** (not 서른 하나 살)
_{seo-leun-han-sal}

When the number 20(**스물**) combines with a counter word, it becomes **스무**.
_{seu-mul} _{seu-mu}

20 years old = **스무 살** (not 스물 살)
_{seu-mu-sal}

For all other numbers, they maintain their original form.

For example,

26 years old = **스물 여섯 살**
_{seu-mul yeo-seot sal}

7 years old = **일곱 살**
_{il-gop sal}

18 years old = **열 여덟 살**
_{yeol yeo-deol sal}

35 years old = **서른 다섯 살**
_{seo-leun da-seot sal}

As you can see, there's no change in the numbers' form, since they end with numbers other than 1, 2, 3 and 4.

Practice Quiz

Write how to say the following in Korean.

1   **5 years old**

_____

2   **14 years old**

_____

3   **21 years old**

_____

4   **47 years old**

_____

5   **32 years old**

_____

6   **"I am 20 years old" in 존댓말?**
        jon-daen-mal

_____

ANSWER

1 다섯 살
      da-seot sal

2 열 네 살
      yeol ne sal

3 스물 한 살
      seu-mul han sal

4 마흔 일곱 살
      ma-heun il-gop sal

5 서른 두 살
      seo-leun du sal

6 저 스무 살이에요. or 저 스무 살입니다.
      jeo seu-mu-sa-li-e-yo   jeo seu-mu-sa-lim-ni-da

A Sino-Korean Numbers

1 Connect each number with the correct Sino-Korean word.

① 1 •   • 이
                               i

② 2 •   • 삼
                               sam

③ 3 •   • 일
                               il

④ 4 •   • 오
                               o

⑤ 5 •   • 사
                               sa

⑥ 6 •   • 육
                               yuk

⑦ 7 •   • 팔
                               pal

⑧ 8 •   • 십
                               sip

⑨ 9 •   • 칠
                               chil

⑩ 10 •   • 구
                               gu

2 What is the correct way to say "35" in Sino-Korean number?

① 삼 오

② 삼십 오

③ 오십 삼

④ 십삼 오

3 Write the number that corresponds to each word.

① 십 칠 = ( )
sip-chil

② 이십 일 = ( )
i-si-bil

③ 사십 육 = ( )
sa-sim-nyuk

④ 팔십 이 = ( )
pal-si-bi

⑤ 구십 삼 = ( )
gu-sip-sam

4 What is the word for "100?"

① 백   ② 천   ③ 만
baek   cheon   man

5 Select one INCORRECT way to read each number.

① 123 = 백 이십 삼

② 202 = 이십백 이

③ 570 = 오백 칠십

④ 468 = 사백 육십 팔

6 What is the word for "1,000?"

① 백   ② 천   ③ 만
baek   cheon   man

7 How would you say each number in Korean? Fill in the blank with the correct Sino-Korean.

① 6,780 = 육(   ) 칠(   ) 팔(   )

② 1,945 = (   ) 구(   ) 사(   ) (   )

8   What is the word for "10,000?"

① 천
cheon

② 십천
sip-cheon

③ 만
man

9   How would you say, "It's 30,000 won?"

(   )이에요.
i-e-yo

10   How do you say, "zero" in Korean?

_____

11   How do you say, "May 8th" in Korean?

_____

12   Listen to the audio and write when the woman's birthday is. (생일 : birthday)
saeng-il

ⓘ **TRACK 103**

Her birthday is on (   ).

Native Korean Numbers

1 Connect each number with the correct native Korean word.

① 1 •		• 다섯 da-seot
② 2 •		• 셋 set
③ 3 •		• 넷 net
④ 4 •		• 하나 ha-na
⑤ 5 •		• 둘 dul

⑥ 6 •		• 열 yeol
⑦ 7 •		• 일곱 il-gop
⑧ 8 •		• 아홉 a-hop
⑨ 9 •		• 여섯 yeo-seot
⑩ 10 •		• 여덟 yeo-deol

2 Connect each number with the correct native Korean word.

① 20 •		• 마흔 ma-heun
② 30 •		• 스물 seu-mul
③ 40 •		• 서른 seo-leun
④ 50 •		• 쉰 shwin
⑤ 60 •		• 예순 ye-sun

3 Write the number that corresponds to each word.

① 열 아홉   = (   )
yeol   a-hop

② 스물 여덟   = (   )
seu-mul yeo-deol

③ 서른 여섯   = (   )
seo-leun yeo-seot

④ 마흔 둘   = (   )
ma-heun dul

4 Select one INCORRET pair.

① 4 years old = 넷 살

② 11 years old = 열 한 살

③ 20 years old = 스무 살

④ 32 years old = 서른 두 살

⑤ 45 years old = 마흔 다섯 살

5 What is the correct way to say "24 years old?"

① 스무 네 살

② 스무 넷 살

③ 스물 네 살

④ 이십 네 살

6 Listen to the audio and fill in the blank with the woman's age.

⊙ TRACK 104

She's (   ) years old.

ANSWER

A

1 ① 일   ② 이   ③ 삼   ④ 사   ⑤ 오
   ⑥ 육   ⑦ 칠   ⑧ 팔   ⑨ 구   ⑩ 십

2 ②

3 ① 17   ② 21   ③ 46   ④ 82   ⑤ 93

4 ①

5 ② (202 = 이백 이)

6 ②

7 ① 천, 백, 십   ② 천, 백, 십, 오

8 ③

9 삼만 원
   sam-ma-nwon

10 영 or 공
   yeong gong

11 5월 8일, or 오월 팔 일
   o wol pa-lil

12 September 16th
   [Audio] 제 생일 구월 십육 일이에요.

B

1 ① 하나   ② 둘   ③ 셋   ④ 넷   ⑤ 다섯
   ⑥ 여섯   ⑦ 일곱   ⑧ 여덟   ⑨ 아홉   ⑩ 열

2 ① 스물   ② 서른   ③ 마흔   ④ 쉰   ⑤ 예순

3 ① 19   ② 28   ③ 36   ④ 42

4 ① (네 살)

5 ③

6 37
   [Audio] 저 서른 일곱 살이에요.

수고 많았어요!

I'm sure you can now read what's written
in Korean handwriting above. It's close to saying
"You did a great job!" in English, but it has
a slightly different connotation. 수고 means "trouble"
or "hard work," and 많았어요 means
"you had many," and it indicates that you worked
diligently and put in a lot of effort.
It's a common word of acknowledgment for someone's
hard work in Korean. You must have put
a lot of time and effort into finishing this book,
and you definitely deserve to hear this.

수고 많았어요!
(Su-go ma-na-sseo-yo!)

Now, armed with a solid foundation and
a better understanding of the Korean language,
I'm sure it will be a valuable asset as you
continue your journey. There's more awaiting
you in the world of Korean, and I hope you
continue to learn many new things as you
advance and one day reach your goal.

Last but not least, thank you for choosing
this book to study Korean. It's my pleasure
to be a part of your learning journey,
and I look forward to being a continued part of it.

— Miss Vicky